TRUE LOVE, AMBITION AND TRAGEDY

Louis J. Papa

Bloomington, IN Milton Keynes, UK

authorHOUSE

AuthorHouse™
1663 Liberty Drive, Suite 200
Bloomington, IN 47403
www.authorhouse.com
Phone: 1-800-839-8640

AuthorHouse™ UK Ltd.
500 Avebury Boulevard
Central Milton Keynes, MK9 2BE
www.authorhouse.co.uk
Phone: 08001974150

First published by AuthorHouse 8/22/2006

ISBN: 1-4259-3318-1 (sc)
ISBN: 1-4259-3317-3 (dj)

Printed in the United States of America
Bloomington, Indiana

This book is printed on acid-free paper.

DEDICATION

This book is dedicated to my darling late wife Teresa. She was my partner, confidant and best friend. She was a great help in accomplishing my successes and gave me most of the happiness in my life.

Table of Contents

PROLOG

This book is my limited biography. My wife asked me to write this book for my children, concentrating on the person they did not really know. Therefore much of my family life which is familiar to them is not included. Aspects of my life are included from my toddler years to well into my retirement years. The struggle I had with extreme bashfulness until I was well into my career at DuPont is highlighted. The two biggest impacts on my life are covered. First, the effect my father had on my development. Then the calming and heartwarming effect my wife had on me. Writing this gave me a better understanding of myself and why I turned out the way I did. I dedicate this book to my wife who helped me greatly to a successful career. Our mutual love always spurred me onward. I had to include some events that help describe her character. I hope this book will give my children and grandchildren a better understanding of my wife and I.

CHAPTER 1

THE EARLY YEARS

I am a third generation Italian-American from South Philadelphia. Three of my grandparents were immigrants who came to this country shortly before 1900. One Grand mother was born in Philly. The three immigrants were naturalized citizens. In my early years our family was what today would be considered lower class. These early years of my life were in the midst of the great depression. Jobs were very difficult to get. Not everyone in our family was employed. As a result we lived in near poverty. My entire family lived in South Philadelphia. During the first year of my life we lived in an apartment. I, of course, do not remember that. Then because of a lack of money we moved into my mother's brother's house at1304 S. 13th street. He was my Uncle Gus and the house was a three story row home. To give a flavor of the neighborhood, one day when I was about four, I went to the corner store to buy treats. The store was two doors away. While there, the local head racketeer sat me on his knee to play with me. I was a cute kid and my mother made me have long curls like Shirley Temple. A couple of minutes after I went home a man came in and shot him to death. Had I not left he may have shot me too. Then a couple of brothers machine gunned a small group of men. Yet, we did not have to lock our doors in that neighborhood. We were always safe.

The next eight years of my life were spent in my uncle's house. My family lived in that home with my uncle's family and my maternal grandmother. This made a total of ten people living there. Largely due to the conditions of the time, things were far from clean. Although at the time they seemed fine. The mattresses were made of a natural material which when mixed with body sweat made an excellent nesting place for bed bugs. Sweat, of course, is a natural occurrence especially during the summer. Air conditioners were not yet available so there was plenty of sweat.

Times were much harder than today. Clothes had to be washed on a scrubbing board using water which was heated on the kitchen gas range. We evidently had no hot water heater, if they even existed at that time. Then the clothes were hung out to dry. In nice weather they were hung outside to dry. But in the winter they were hung in the house creating an unhealthy atmosphere. Water also had to be heated on the kitchen stove for baths as well as for washing clothes. Thus no one bathed or washed their hair or clothes near as often as they do today. These conditions created an every Friday evening ritual I will never forget. It was the hunt for head lice. I still remember my mom running the fine tooth comb through my hair to remove those nasty critters and their nits. These conditions combined with a house that was cold in the winter and hot in the summer made everyone sick often.

Our heat was generated by a coal burning furnace. It consisted of hot water circulating through room radiators. Either the heating system was inadequate, the house was poorly insulated or both. The house was always cold during the winter. I remember the family always gathering near the kitchen range's lit gas jets to get warm. It's no wonder I was sick so often. As I look back on those days it's a wonder any of us kids or moms survived. The husbands never seemed to get sick. Maybe because they were not home much. In spite of these early hardships there was a lot of limited family togetherness. By limited I refer to my father not being home very often. The togetherness was with my mom's family.

When I was about five years old my mom's mother died. Then about a year later my uncle passed away from a heart attack. He was only about fifty-two years old. He was a nice man. I remember we both liked each other. He was like a father to me. He sat me on his lap and played with me often. We found out later it was not the hard life that killed him. His three sons lived a much better life than he did. But each of them died of heart attacks in their early fifties too. So, it must have been genetic. I was fortunate enough to survive my many illnesses and went on to live a happy life in my adulthood.

However my life did seem to be an endless struggle sprinkled with many good times after I met my wife. Between these sprinkles it seemed almost like running a hurdle race through most of my years. There always appeared to be one hurdle after another. It is certainly true that many of these hurdles were created by me but nonetheless they were there as obstacles to overcome. Almost all people have a series of obstacles in their lives too. But either because they actually were worse than others or because they were happening to me, mine seemed more difficult. Some of these hurdles were high and some were low. But regardless of their size they were present and loomed sometimes as giant obstacles.

I do not remember much else of my early years but a few things do stand out. I think my earliest years were spent as a mama's boy even though my curls made me look like a girl. My mother and I were always very close. Remember I was all she had to comfort her most of the time. She was very young, giving birth to me at seventeen, and her husband was rarely home. In my late teens, I evolved as her protector. Despite our closeness I never remember my mom taking me out in the world as other mothers do with their children. I do not remember such things as walks in the park or even to see Santa Claus at Christmas time. She may have done it when I was too young to remember, but I doubt it. I doubt it because in later years I do not remember her doing it with my younger brothers or sister either. But, because I was a good deal older I was not home much then. I can only remember her taking me to two movies when I was about 6-7 years old. One was "GONE WITH THE WIND" and all I remember about the other is John Garfield was the star.

As was the custom back then, men ruled the family. Wives were treated almost like slaves. The men rarely or never helped their wives. My father was no exception. Even at this young age I began to feel sorry for women. All our family events were with my father's side of the family. I do not remember spending one holiday with my mom's family even when we lived with them. His family events were also the only time we went out as a family. They were generally holiday dinners or special gatherings. I wonder now how my mother could stand being isolated from her family. His family was fun though and I enjoyed being with them. My memories of going out for youngster type entertainment, such as seeing Christmas decorations in Department Stores, Santa Claus and various other kid's sights were always with my father's mother.

By the time I was five my mother's mom was dead. About then my other grandmother started taking me places. She was a fun woman all the time I knew her. That was up until I was in my forties and she was in her eighties. When she took me out as a small boy, she always tried to hide her age. She would insist that I call her Aunt Molly rather than Grand mom. We always went out with her friend Suzy. My Grand mom would tell me to call her aunt. Little me, would say in a cute diminutive voice, "You're not my aunt, you're my Grand mom." This always made them chuckle. I really enjoyed the trips with her. Not only because they were my only outings, but they always included a stop at the Horn & Hardart's Automat. My mom never took me out to eat anywhere that I can remember. But the automat was my favorite place. I loved to eat there. The Automat trips were a real treat to me. Like a real kid I thought it was neat to pick out your food, put the money in the slot, turn the handle and get it out of it's glass cage. Also, I loved their pot of baked beans. Unfortunately, trips with Grand mom were very limited because she worked full time. So other than Grand mom's trips my contacts with the outside world were limited to school, playing with kids and movies with friends or my cousins.

Probably this lack of getting out in the world and meeting people hindered my social development. I think it made me a bit backward too. I certainly was backward and underdeveloped socially as a youngster. These traits coupled with my most serious shortcoming, extreme shyness, made much of life difficult for me. The shyness haunted me most of my life. As an example of how bad it was for me in the beginning. Back at about age three I remember burying my face in my mother's lap whenever people were visiting. I would keep it there and was too shy to look at the visitors for the entire time that they were there. It did not matter how long they stayed, I would stay buried in her lap. This would cause pains in my neck if they stayed too long, but I would not lift my head. It was always a painful experience for me, but I did it every time, anyway. It sure sounds dumb to me now.

This combination of traits haunted me most of my life. It was especially damaging when I had to give talks. This happened to a limited extent in Jr. and Sr. high school. Then it occurred much more frequently in graduate school. Also, I gave what I now consider poor talks on my job interviews and during my early years at work. I seemed to hide my shyness and other bad traits as the years passed on to adulthood. My guess, is I unknowingly developed methods to hide or cover my shyness and underdeveloped social skills as a young teenager. These were new traits like sarcasm and using my quick wit. The sarcasm I developed when coupled with my quick wit was evidently offensive to some people. These traits lingered throughout my married life. Many times my wife told me of possibly offending people. But by now it was an ingrained habit and a part of my nature that was difficult to break. These traits may have often made people think I was a rude, wise guy. This was never my intention or wish. When I hear that criticism leveled at me today, it's hard for me to believe I offended people. The quick wit takes over and the words flow out like gumballs from a machine. But I keep trying even at my advanced age.

There is no doubt that the dominate feature of my memories as a young person is a father that was never around for my mother or any of his children. As a result, I spent most of my life trying to get recognition and an expression of love from him. I never got either. He never gave my mother or me and later my siblings much attention. I assume the same was true of my siblings when I got married and left home. He certainly never did when I lived there. When I was old enough to understand the ways of the world, I knew him as a womanizer, drinker, gambler and a mafia want-to-be. He did seem to have some sort of minor connections with the "mob". His treatment of women in general and my mother in particular was true to the older Italian men's philosophy of how to treat a woman. Their saying was that a woman is like a broom. You keep her in the closet till you need her, then take her out and use her. You put her back when you are done. I heard that from the older Italian men many times. This philosophy always angered me. It may have been my mother's influence but women were always special to me.

On the other hand my mother was an overly timid person that continually took abuse until pushed to her limit. Then she over-reacted. Trouble was her boiling point was too high. She accepted my dad's non-family man macho behavior. She turned her back to much of his unacceptable behavior that she HAD to know he did. I could never understand why she put up with him. His treatment of her made me love her more and want to protect her. I often thought she should have had "welcome" stamped on her back the way she let him step all over her. She lived life almost like a hermit or recluse. Not only did she very rarely take me or her other children out but she rarely went out herself. She seemed content to sit home and do puzzles. During my teen years I did all of the food shopping for her. She did not even go out to food shop. Later my siblings inherited that job. During my pre- and early school years my parents' relationship did not catch my attention very often. I was just too young to notice such things. As I got older what I considered their incompatibility became very noticeable to me. It was not so much their incompatibility as it was his treatment of any woman. You could just tell he regarded them as toys for his pleasure.

Other things occupied my attention when I was young. Playing and making noise were high on my list. Because I was alone so often might be the reason for my self reliance. At the same time this did nothing to help my shyness. Things began to happen in the world which would occupy my attention. In my first year of school the Japanese attacked Pearl Harbor. The fall-out from this act occupied my attention for years. All the young men of the neighborhood and our family either enlisted or were drafted. Some never came back. Even at my young age this impacted me. I still remember the heartache the women suffered during those years. This reinforced my feelings toward women. Missing in action and killed in action flags were in many windows. All of us kids endured scary things, for us, like blackouts periodically. These were actually practice for air raids should they occur. They presented no real danger but no one told us kids. My dad managed to not go in the service. Although I did not want to see him hurt, I was not proud that my father deliberately avoided it.

Times were scary for us young kids. The black-outs were common. We kids were made to think they could really be air raids. I grew to know their significance from movies and movie newsreels. Movies are probably the thing that made me so aware of the situation and so sympathetic to the women left alone or who lost their men. Although I did not want my father to be killed like these men, it still bothered me that he found a way out while all the other men were enlisting. The war was an especially scary time for most kids. I know it had a big impact on me. As the war dragged on for about the third year, some women got overly lonely. Even though their husbands were away for a couple of years, they got pregnant. One of my aunts was one of those women.

This was the nature of the times during my earliest years at school. Despite this, I was evidently a very good student, anyway. In my second year of school, illness struck me. I missed most of the semester with whopping cough. I remember my mother spending many hours at the bedside with me. My father never seemed to be around the house even when we needed him. In those days, due to a teacher shortage, the school terms were divided in half with the teacher spending half a day with each set of students. The halves were labeled A and B. In the second grade I missed almost the entire A semester due to the whooping cough.

My mother was naturally concerned about my status at school. So mom visited my teacher. The trip was to see if the teacher planned to leave me back. Much to my mom's surprise the teacher expressed her happiness with my progress to that point. The teacher labeled me her best student by far. She had been considering having me skipped a half grade. But now, any advancement of that sort would have to await further review. They would have to evaluate my continued progress upon my return. My 2B semester return must have been spectacular. This was aided, of course, by the teacher shortage which created the need to teach two half grades simultaneously. The A & B students were taught half a day each in the same classroom. My class was made up of 2B & 3A. I could still remember listening intently to the other grade's work after I finished mine. Thanks to my good memory I would absorb both teachings and often was the only student who could answer 3A questions even though I was in 2B. The result was the teacher or school administrators skipped me to 3B. This move showed no effect on me scholastically. I easily adapted to the work. But later it would show up in high school as a lack of maturity especially in relationships with girls.

Though my memories are scant, a few do stick in my mind from those early years. Again they are related to a father rarely spending time with us or somehow disappointing me. In my mind he certainly *never* did anything for me or my mother. One instance that stands out in my mind for some reason occurred during World War II. My school was having a drive to collect expired license plates to get scrap metal for the war effort. As a concerned child, this donation was very important to me to contribute to the war effort. I had seen all the war movies and now had my chance to help defeat the dreaded Germans and Japs. After seeing them in movies I would do anything to beat them.

When the school had a scrap metal drive, I had my chance to contribute. Accordingly, I asked my dad every time we met to try to get some auto license plates for me to donate. He promised me over and over again that he would get them for me. But they somehow never arrived. Like most kids I kept pestering him for them. He persisted in promising to get them for me. The drive lasted about three months. Toward the end of the drive I begged him to get them. This time he solemnly promised to get them. The drive ended without any contribution from me. Eventually I forgot about the plates and the drive as time passed. Then about a month or two after the drive had ended he popped up with the plates. He acted like it was a big surprise for me. I could still see him at the front door with the plates in his hands. Disappointment quickly showed on his face when he entered the door and learned the time had elapsed. The look on his face impacted my memory. That is why I probably remember this incident. I remember actually feeling sorry for him. It must have been youth or inherited genes of my mother. It was obvious he wanted to get the plates for me but other things must have had a higher priority. This was the beginning of my learning just how much I could depend on my father.

As the years past I got out of having to play alone all the time. I spent most of my time playing with my two cousins, Junior and Artie, and going to war and cowboy movies with them. All we saw were those two types of movies. We played with toy guns all the time. We three cousins were inseparable buddies and had lots of fun together. In those days the entire family lived close to each other so my cousins lived nearby. This was true of most families in South Philly back then. Present times are not the same. Between moving far away and having a mother who hid from her family because she was ashamed of my father, I have not seen my cousins since I was nine years old. Our family togetherness was destroyed. Recently an unknown cousin called my mother to let her know her brother Art had died. I answered the phone in my mother's absence As it turned out it was Artie's brother. Until then, I did not know he had a brother.

Despite my parents continual fighting and problems getting along with each other, my mother somehow managed to get pregnant. When her pregnancy ended she had a baby girl. I was eight years old at the time. My father named her Amalia after his mother as I was named after his father. My mother had no say in the matter. Like most older brothers I was proud to have a little sister. She was a cute little girl but soon would grow up to be a walking terror. By that I mean she was always making kid type trouble. There was never anything malicious.

Now I was getting old enough to more clearly see problems between my mom and dad. As I got older the problems were becoming more evident to me. Those problems were soon over shadowed by a larger one. My dad worked at the Naval Shipyard in Philadelphia. This is how he avoided the service. His management transferred him to the San Francisco yard. Moves of that distance were unheard of in those days. This was especially true for South Philly Italians. My guess is his superiors probably wanted to get rid of him. He was running a little side business on the ships. They probably discovered that he was supplying the sailors with liquor that was forbidden to them. In return the sailors would supply him with the hard to get rationed food and cigarettes that were plentiful on the war ships. They obviously stole all these items from the abundant supplies on the ships. These items were rationed to the general population to supply the service men. So now my dad had slabs of bacon, coffee, steaks, all the food people wanted badly and cigarettes for the addicts. He was now a big deal having all the hard-to-get items that were rationed to the general population. This made him a hit with everyone, especially people who smoked. He undoubtedly sold some of the items too. I was nine years old and knew this. Somehow that knowledge evaded my mother. At least she would not admit to knowing it.

Rather than being fired and drafted into the service he reluctantly took the move to Frisco. Avoiding the draft is the reason he worked at the yard in the first place. When the time came to leave, he purchased a drawing room on a train to Frisco so he could have his comfort and privacy. My mom and dad's plan was to have us join him after he established housing in Frisco. This process took a good deal longer than we expected. But well before he left, my mother had done it for a third time. She was pregnant again. A few months later my fully blossoming mother, my sister and I traveled coach on a train to join him. I still remember that she had to go coach in her condition whereas he had his own room. As usual, he found money for his pleasure.

These are the beginnings from which I evolved. It was an uneducated family from a lower class neighborhood. We kids had a father who was that in name only. We had a mother who was a timid recluse. In reviewing all the events of my early life to write this book I developed a better understanding of myself. With hard work and an exceptional partner I overcame all of this and went on to have a successful and happy life.

CHAPTER 2

LIFE ON THE WEST COAST

The first thing I remember about the West Coast is a long five day train ride. It was a real adventure for a nine year old boy. I thought it was neat to eat every meal in the dining car. It was an elegant restaurant on wheels. Crossing first the Mississippi river then the Great Salt Lake in Utah stands out in my mind. The river because it's name made it well known. But the lake is the most dominant in my memory. This is because all the talk on the train was of it's size. Well before we reached it the talk about the lake intensified. The talk interested me because I was always afraid of water and could not swim. So, the crossing had me afraid at first. But after hearing many passengers say there was so much salt in it that a person could not sink. This alleviated my fears at first. But as we crossed the large body of water, the train seemed almost the same width as the bridge. This rekindled my fear. Then I began to wonder if the train would float too. Somehow I knew it would sink with me in it. Crossing it seemed endless to me. The experience was frightening. But relief set in when we finished the crossing.

That memory stands out in my mind but there are others. Among these was the preparation for sleeping. Beds called upper births were dropped from the ceiling. Happily we kids got to climb up and sleep in them. To me this was a real treat. You could climb up into bed. One night disaster struck. My sister fell out of her upper birth while asleep. She banged her head rather hard. She did a good deal of screaming and crying. The porter came running but fortunately Molly was not badly injured. The porter became very friendly to us thereafter. He paid attention mainly to my sister, who seemed to catch his fancy. She struck up a close friendship with this man. My sister became someone who he seemed to adore. He was a black man. Whites and blacks did not associate very much back then. But we were kids. We did not know about such things. All we knew was that he was a very nice man. As I remember we liked him very much. We enjoyed his company throughout the trip and he played with my sister often and made us have lots of fun. But the train finally reached Frisco and we could begin our new adventure.

Almost from the moment we got off the train I felt like we were entering a new world. The first big difference I noticed was that their streets had many steep hills. Their trolley cars looked very different to me. I was told that they were not actually trolleys. They were cable cars. The hills were so steep that a cable was necessary to pull the cars up the hills. The scenery on the way to our home was simply beautiful. The homes were quite different from the Philly row homes that I knew. Later we toured the countryside and saw more breathe taking sights. It even impressed me, just a youngster. It was a shame I was not older. Then I would have appreciated it even more. Top off these niceties with super weather like Philadelphia has only on its nicest spring and fall days. These facts made the west coast hard to beat.

Our new home was 804 Lathrop Ave. At that time, it was a government project for the workers at the Frisco yard. The change of residence did mean a new school for me. My parents enrolled me in the Candlestick Cove elementary school. The area was called Candlestick Cove. Later this area would become the site of Candlestick Park, the home of the San Francisco Giants Major League baseball team. Most of the families in the project were from the hills of the deep south, the southwest or California. The schools in their home towns were behind the Philadelphia schools. Quickly, I became happy with my new school when I learned that the school and the students were well behind my former school in Philadelphia. All the students and the school in my grade level were well behind my training level. This made me a star student. Just about all of the students were well behind my training level. This made the work much easier for me. With my good memory it was mostly a review for me. Suddenly I was a star in the eyes of the class and the teacher. All the students came to me for help.

Probably the thing I remember most about our time on the West Coast was the closest we ever had to a normal family life. All the rest of the time my family was dysfunctional mainly due to the relationship between my parents. But that seemed to get calmer during our stay in Frisco. My dad was home regularly. My mom was happier than back in Philly. Shortly after we settled in our Frisco home, my mom gave birth to the baby she carried on the train. It was a baby boy. My father named him John after squabbling with my mother. She wanted to name him Robert. As usual my father ruled. The name was selected to honor my uncle, the pharmacist. This move was undoubtedly made to extract favors or money in the future. I was only ten years old but I remember my father forcing the name on my mother. It was not the name she would have chosen. But she had no say in the matter, after all, she only carried him and gave birth.

My years in Frisco were memorable for me. Things that stand out in my mind were the roller coasters the kids got for Christmas. These items were copies of our East Coast sleds. They were similar in every way except they had wheels instead of runners. This was a necessity in the Frisco climate. It almost never snowed there. It did not even get cold in the winter. The kids used them in the same way we used sleds. They took "belly flops" down hills and the coasters rolled forever. In that respect they were better than sleds for kids to have fun. But since they rolled so far it was probably hazardous.

One unforgettable event occurred when several of my friends and I were playing on the wreckage of an old ship on the shore of the bay. It was partially on land but mostly in the bay. We took a row boat out to where we could climb onto the wreck. Another boy and I struggled to be first out of the boat and onto the wreck. He won the race and I was pushed into the San Francisco bay. The bay got deep quickly. The water was over my head. As mentioned earlier, I could not swim and was afraid of water. I thought that drowning was for sure. But luckily, I stayed afloat until one of the guys pushed the row boat near me to grab. Grab onto it I did, until my playmates could help me get on the wreck. One of the moccasins on my feet got lost in the bay as a result of my dip. So with one shoe on and one shoe off I went hobbling home. It must have really been a sight to see a kid hobbling down the street with only one shoe on and thoroughly soaked. Not being sure what awaited me at home, I began to cry. Could you picture me showing up at my front door crying and a one-shoed dripping wet kid. That's the sight that greeted my mother when she opened the door. As one would expect she was shocked.

I also remember meeting people from all over the country who were very different from my norm. The teenagers were obsessed with sex. The boys were all bragging that they were getting it. The town was crawling with women looking for men. The large number of sailors attracted them. The whole town was sex crazed. I did not know much about sex then but I knew enough to realize what was happening. Two friends of mine from Oklahoma, ages about 9 and 10, were thrilled one night that it was "titty night". They responded to my request of what's that? They told me that's the night we get to play with mom's titties. Even at my young age I thought that was strange. I could not even conceive of seeing my mom's breasts bare let alone playing with them. They must have had some mom.

Another memory was created by my devilish sister. She messed up the house every morning before my parents awoke. They were late risers and sound sleepers. My father had a "bright idea". Her room and the bathroom were at right angles to each other. So to stop her antics my dad decided to tie the two door knobs to each other. His plan was to keep her locked in the room so she could not get out, but he did leave only enough slack in the rope for her to call if she needed them. At least that's what he thought. But he used clothes line rope. In the morning the terror tried to pull her door open. The rope stretched too much or my dad left a little too much slack in the line. She was strong enough to stretch the rope. The rope stretched just enough for her to stick her head in the space that was created. When she let go of the door, the rope tightened, and the door clamped on her head. There she was stuck in the door. In that position she could not open it or move her head. The pressure placed on the head hurt her. We all woke up to her screaming with her head stuck in the door. We felt guilty to laugh at this scene but it was a funny sight.

Then how could I ever forget my first girlfriend. She was a freckled face, cute, blonde haired girl named Mary Lou Mason. Only I knew she was my girlfriend. She never found out. I was too shy to tell her. It was probably her name I liked more than her anyway. My memories of our time in Frisco are good. We had a family life and I had fun. The only thing wrong with our stay was that it was too short. But this was another step in forming who I am.

CHAPTER 3

RETURNING HOME

The long war had finally ended. The need for building new warships was about finished. Repair of the ships in service slowly ended too. Thus my dad's job which was machining gun turrets came to an end. My family now returned home courtesy of my uncle John. This was probably the first dividend for naming my brother after him. The first order of business was to find a place to live. But we needed a temporary residence until my parents could find something permanent. My father's naming of his son now paid another dividend. His sister and her husband John took us into their drugstore/home until more permanent accommodations could be found. This meant a new school for me again. This would be my third in a little over a year. It would also be my fifth residence in ten years. My parents enrolled me in the Ethan Allen elementary school. Like any young kid I quickly made friends and got comfortable in the new school. My dad found a job too. It was as a used car salesman in the lot across from my uncle's store.

We were not at my uncle's home long before the terror struck. One morning while everyone was still asleep Molly found an iron. She decided to act like a mom and do some ironing. She plugged it into an electrical outlet. Then as kids will do she walked away when something else caught her attention. But the iron was left connected to the outlet. It was on a rug atop a wooden floor. It heated up and slowly burned right through the carpet then began burning through the wood. Luckily my uncle had just awakened to open his store. While he was getting dressed, the burning smell caught his attention. He traced it to the iron just before it completely burned through to the first floor. He later told us the handle was very hot. So he removed the plug then picked it up with his bare hand and threw it aside. In the process he received minor burns. The resulting damage was a hole in the carpet and the floor that looked like someone carved the shape of an iron. Thank goodness he woke up when he did or this story may have ended here. This was my third brush with death.

As time passed, the need for privacy grew in both families. Living alone was missed by each family. There were no hostilities but the families longed for their privacy. So my parents began house hunting. After a few months they found and purchased a house ay 6329 Marsden Street. Now I would have six different residences in ten years. The home was in a neighboring school district. So this would mean another new school for me. This did not please me at all. By now I was deeply entrenched with friends at Allen. The age had been reached where friends count more than anything else. I did not want to leave Allen. But Allen was only a little over a mile from our new home. At my request my parents negotiated with the school authorities and got special permission for me to remain at Allen. The only stipulation was for me to get there without the school's assistance. Even with that distance I elected to do the walking to and from Allen rather than change schools. The walk was only difficult for me in the winter when it was cold and windy. But I did not mind as long as I had my friends.

As time progressed two factors were at play that became related. My grandmother began to worry about my father's old age since he had no pension. Simultaneously her sister, Dora, was having trouble getting maintenance on her two apartment buildings in Wildwood NJ. My grandmother and her daughter came up with an idea which would solve both problems. My father was to help his aunt by maintaining her two rental buildings. In return, she would leave them to him when she died. Since she never had children this would not create a problem. At first my dad balked at the idea. He had a good paying, easy job as a used car salesman. He would not be paid much by his aunt but could live there free. He felt why should he give up his easy, good paying job. This move supposedly was going to benefit both Aunt Dora and my dad. So all the women teamed up and launched a relentless sustained attack of nagging him. A year or two later my dad surrendered. My parents sold their house in preparation for their move to the resort town. Now I was sure of another residence and another school change. This did not make me happy. But this was an ill conceived plan from the beginning. Everyone should have known my dad was not suited to do heavy physical work. Little me knew that. The grown ups should have known too. Regardless we made the move.

When we arrived in Wildwood, we immediately ran into an obstacle. The resort town did not have the A, B system in their school that Philadelphia did. Their system only had full years. The school authorities reviewed my situation and were unyielding in not moving me up another half grade. Their plan was that if I transferred they would drop me back the one semester I had gained. They argued, and as it turned out, rightly so, the immaturity difference would be too great. This was unacceptable to my parents. If they had their way I would not have liked girls till after high school, anyway. But they were equally rigid about keeping my semester gain. They felt my reward for hard work should not be taken away. So they left me in Allen and arranged for me to go back to live with my aunt and uncle who lived in the Allen school district. This would be my seventh move but with no school change this time. I would be in Philly and my mom and dad would be in

Wildwood. No one asked me for my preference. I would have rather been with my mother and got left back.

Due to the separation my grandmother took me on train rides most weekends to visit my mom and dad. I looked forward to the rides there with great anticipation. Mom and I would both cry when I had to return. The trips back were miserable since I would cry most of the return trip. Like I said earlier no one ever asked me if I would rather do this or be left back. Even though my friends were at Allen, I would have rather been with my mom. I really did not care where my father lived. Although it was not my first choice at least this new setup would keep me with my friends.

But this move had it's downside. I was stuck living with an aunt who was not my favorite person, although I really liked my uncle. My aunt would always ask one of her daughters to do a chore and usually they would find a way not to do it. Somehow it would always wind up on my shoulders. If I did not do it my sneaky aunt would let my father know about it. This would lead to a punishment for me. So living there was like the story of Cinderella and her two step-sisters with me being Cindy. Only there was no prince to rescue me.

My aunt was everything for show. Religion was a good example. She acted like it was an important thing in her life. However, when she was away from home she rarely went to church on Sunday. When she was home it was a different story. My aunt and uncle had a lot of friends who were priests in their parish. The priests came to their house often for coffee. So, at home where the priests could see her, she went to mass every Sunday. But they could not see her when she was out of town, so she rarely went. I always thought her religion thing was just for show. But she got carried away and acted like it was important to me too. My mom was a convert by force. She and dad never went to church therefore so neither did I. Yet my meddling aunt enrolled me for religious instructions to get my First Holy Communion and Confirmation. This would be my first contact with the church. I had never even been in one up until then. She had to show the priests. To me it was another chore that was on my aunt's list. But I had to obey her every wish. If not she would sneakily tell my father. That would always lead to a punishment for me.

The church for my instructions was across the street from my school. While teaching me the nuns must have done a good job of brainwashing me. The job was so good that for a short period of time I became an avid catholic. I actually attended mass every day before school. A memory of an incident that occurred in the era when I was attending Allen while getting the instructions lingers. It revolves around this religious training. A boy wanted to fight me in school one day. I used the excuse that the Sister at the church taught me it was a sin to fight. I truly believed this but have to admit I was somewhat afraid since he was a good deal bigger than me. At any rate he got enraged that I would not fight him. He took a swing at me anyway. The blow struck me on the head. The boy immediately stopped. He was obviously in great pain. The blow to my head had broken his finger. This brought on comments from my friends like that's using your head, Lou. This event caused me to think maybe there was something to this religion thing after all.

As expected, my father gave up maintaining his aunt's buildings. He figured his aunt could live too long to make his work worth it. The job did not pay enough and he had to get a night job at a gas station as well. The work was too hard and boring for him. His time being so occupied cut into his carousing. So he moved back to Philly without my mother and became a fast-talking used car salesman again that rips off people. He got his job back at the car lot across the street from my aunt and uncle's house/drugstore. At least he was in the right element now. Now without my mom around, he could drink and carouse all he wished. During the rest of my years at Allen, with no mother at home and a father that did not care, I was not very happy and became a minor behavior problem at school. That ended about when school ended. The school year ended and graduation came. No one from my family attended. My mother was in Wildwood and my father was who knows where. I felt humiliated. All my friends had their parents there and I had to sit all alone. It was embarrassing. A couple of the teachers who knew my mother was away saw me all alone. Fortunately for me they came to sit with me. That was a relief. Now I had jumped the first low hurdle in my life. All kids look forward to the hurdle of finishing elementary school.

Right after the graduation my mother came back to live with us. My parents got an apartment in central Mayfair. This would be my eighth move. Now I would start attendance at Woodrow Wilson Jr. High School. I would only be in Wilson for one year. My stay there would be marked by continued mediocrity of grades. For a short time I became a wise guy. I remember spending every spring lunch time at Wilson watching softball games. There was a super player named Albrecht that was worth watching. He hit home runs out of the school yard often. I never got the chance to meet him. Later in life, his son and my youngest son would turn out to be best friends. They were best men at each other's weddings and godfather for each other's first-born child. I met Mr. Albrecht at my son's wedding. Life sure has unexpected twists.

Our new apartment was on the 7200 block of Frankford Avenue. It was not very nice but now that I had my mother back. I was happy and my behavior problems ended. Our apartment was located next to an eat-in bar, which caused roach infestation. The roaches freaked out my mother. She kept harping on my father to move. Finally he gave in and bought a new house. To make this purchase he needed his mother to co-sign for the mortgage. This bothered him a great deal. He made much more money than she did so he thought his signature should be enough. But as a car salesman his salary was unreliable and volatile. Though smaller, her salary was dependable. So we moved into the new home. It was in the same school district as Wilson so I did not have to change schools. This would now be my ninth residence. Life at the new house was exciting. All things were clean and new which made life a lot nicer.

I made many new friends rapidly in the new neighborhood. We all continually played many street ball games of just about every type. This was great for me. My parents made friends with the neighbors too. We were like a family at last. For the first time my mother seemed to come out of her shell. She and my dad were meeting nightly with all the new neighbors. The women of the immediate neighborhood started a canasta club. It was good to see my mom having fun with people for the first time in my memory. My father and the men started a credit union. It was illegal to do that but they did it anyway. They made my dad treasurer. I was sure this was a bad move on their part.

The novelty of the new neighborhood ended. My dad got back to his old ways. The fighting between my parents started again. Either it got worse or being older now I was more aware. In bed at night I would hear them fighting and him handing out verbal abuse. It usually centered around his drinking and never being home or coming home very late.

That was the kind of abusive relationship I witnessed. I never saw or heard any physical abuse. But there was some minor physical abuse. These goings on happened many nights. I remember vowing many times to always treat my wife like a queen when I get married. If I had children, I vowed to be a good father and do things with them. This vow was made so many times to myself that it became plastered in my brain. This was because I heard his abuse so often.

My school year progressed with only one further noteworthy event. In English class I had a very good teacher. One day we had to give a talk on a recent movie we saw, I said unprepared rather than stand before the class and talk. He realized why I did it. So he decided to break me of it. Then he asked what movie did I see last. When I responded THE MONTE STRATTON STORY, he said well tell us about it. I reluctantly got up to talk. I felt so dizzy I saw stars or bright colored spots before my eyes. I also felt so weak in the knees that I almost passed out. I remember feeling the room spinning around. My tongue either swelled or felt like it was swelling. I fumbled my words. That's how shy I was in front of an audience. But he made me do it. He knew what my problem was and tried to make me overcome it. And so I survived my first stand up talk.

Graduation from Wilson came. I remember sitting on the stage and scanning the audience. My eyes found my mother but no father. Dad had missed my second graduation. It was embarrassing to have my friends know he was a no-show again. Many of my fellow students graduated with me from Allen. They knew he did not show up at that one either. The second low hurdle of my life was passed. Again it was not a big deal but something every kid looks forward to with anticipation. Only I expected that both my parents would be there to share it with me.

CHAPTER 4

The High School Years

By the time my High School days were about to begin I was a complete nut over most sports. My main interest was baseball with football running a close second. My secret dream was to play varsity football and baseball for my high school. Then in my mind was the fantasy that I would be good enough to go on to the professionals in baseball. In football I thought I could kick good enough to make most college teams. But those were the days before specialists. I was not good enough to play offense or defense. My serious drawback in both sports was a lack of foot speed. But I was enough of a realist to know that playing professional baseball was extremely unlikely. Deep down I knew that I was not good enough. Hell, I would be lucky to make the high school team. Like most kids my dreams did not live up to reality. The professionals were just a figment of my imagination. As it turned out my sports career would be limited to the sandlots with a year of semi-pro baseball.

Being a Wilson graduate I was automatically enrolled at the school in my district. All I had to do was show up on opening day. I was in the district of the newly built Lincoln High School. The first day the school opened its doors, I was there. Being in a modern new school was a thrill to me. Lincoln had all the new innovations of the time. In the main halls there were ramps to go to the second floor. The school also had stairs on the outer perimeter. They were for students or teachers to use if they were in the vicinity of the stairs and had the desire to use them. They were undoubtedly also there in case of a fire. Although there was a choice, almost all the students and faculty used the ramps. You might say it was the first step for America's youth to no longer exercise. The school was beautiful and I was going to be in the first class that had gone all the way through the senior high school starting from after Jr. High school.

My high school years were an enjoyable time for me from the first day. Many of my friends attended Lincoln. About one third of Wilson's graduating class and all of my Allen graduating class were there. So I was surrounded by friends. In addition the upper class students and the faculty members were all very friendly. Everything considered, it was a tight knit community. All the ingredients were present from the beginning for a good stay. The school even had a community room with a juke box for dancing at lunch time. My shyness and having two left feet made me afraid to even try, so I never learned to dance. I was a late bloomer and had no interest in girls yet. I did not recognize that it was important to females to be able to dance. Also I never gave it a thought that some day soon I would desire girls. Then knowing how to dance would be an asset. The lack of maturity from skipping was now beginning to show. I was a year younger than most of my class mates. My shyness and late blooming were also contributing.

Lincoln was built on one of the neighborhood ball fields where I had played sandlot baseball. This helped spur my dream of playing baseball there. I was a very good hitter back then with what some described as a picture perfect swing. My swing got many compliments from other kids and coaches. My hopes to make the varsity team hinged on my swing and a strong, accurate throwing arm. From the outfield I could throw further with more velocity and accuracy than any kid in the school. Luckily I was a left-handed hitter. This put me closer to first base and helped my serious drawback of a lack of speed as a runner. You might say I waddled like a duck. My father had deliberately made me left-handed to be like his favorite player, Lefty O'Doul. Although this move aided my lack of speed for running to first base, I was still too slow. Unfortunately, being left-handed limited my possible playing positions to outfield, first base or pitcher. My throwing arm was stronger and more accurate than any kid in the area. My arm was befitting a Major Leaguer. I often threw out base runners from the outfield. This skill made me an ideal candidate for the outfield but my lack of foot speed made me a poor choice for that position. I liked and was well suited for catcher. But no one would let left-handers catch. Coaches would not hear of it. Even now I can not understand why. As a first baseman I was a fairly good fielder but most coaches insisted I was too short. That made a poor target for the other infielders. Also I could not stretch as far as a taller player could. The only position remaining for me was pitcher, which I dearly loved anyway.

If I could choose a position to play, my first two choices would have been pitcher or catcher. That way your always in the action of the game. You could use your head to out-smart or out-guess the batters. That was the part of the game I liked best. My strong arm should have had me a good pitcher or catcher. Since catcher was ruled out by all coaches that left only pitcher which was my favorite position anyway. Because of my strong arm I expected to have a very good fastball. But somehow it was not there. My fastball was less than mediocre. It used to make me angry. I could not understand it. Players with much weaker arms from the outfield than mine had better fastballs as a pitcher than I did. The only plausible explanation was improper technique. Recently, at age 65, I found a possible reason. While watching a Phillies game, Larry Andersen a former Major League pitcher, said the tighter you grip the ball the slower you throw it and the looser you grip it the faster you throw it. I always gripped it tight. In fact my entire hand tightly gripped the ball when I threw a curve ball. This was so I could get a lot of spin on it. Recently I saw on TV that many professional pitchers throw change-ups by gripping the ball tightly with their entire hand. It's all clear to me now. All of this explains why I had a good change-up curve and not a good fast ball. When I threw from the outfield there was not time to grip the ball tightly so I held it loosely and made a fast throw. I probably did not use my legs to push off properly, either. With this knowledge I may have been a really good pitcher.

So maybe that was the answer to my absent fast ball. No one ever taught me how to do it correctly when I played. Without a good fastball most coaches especially the professionals would not even consider a man as pitcher. But the accuracy of my throwing arm gave me very good control. I almost never walked anyone. Being a smart pitcher saved me. Without a fastball I learned a lot of junk pitches like the over-the-hill major league pitchers do. I only used my fast ball to show hitters and keep them off-balance. The first pitch I ever threw was a fast ball in the strike zone. The batter hit it out of sight. Fortunately it was foul. But I never threw one in the strike zone again. Opposing teams would beg me to throw the fast one over the plate. I did have a very good slow curve ball. In my very first pitching performance in semi-pro ball I got a visit from our catcher in the first inning. He had been in the professional minor leagues. He came out to the mound and said, "Lou you have the best change-up curve ball I have ever seen. But you have nothing to change-up from." That was the end of my semi-pro pitching career. I did stay the rest of the year to play first base and outfield. My pitching career was then limited to sandlots. In that league I was a very successful pitcher and outfielder. I did make the Junior Varsity high school team as an outfielder. I proudly earned a letter. However my pitching remained confined to the sandlots.

Unfortunately my playing days for the school came to an abrupt halt. My dreams were crushed. To this day the reason angers me because the football team won the public league championship in my senior year. I played with one of the team's best defensive players in the sandlot league and just knew I could have made the team as a linebacker or defensive end. But during that summer my father did one of his disappearing acts. He just took off to go to Florida. I believe his quote that got back to me later was "I'm going to see the Cuba girls". This poor excuse for a father and husband abandoned my mother and his children. Ashamed, my mother went back into her shell. She dropped all relations with our neighbors.

This immediately created a problem. The concerned close relatives had to devise a way to support his family and not let us starve. To keep us afloat my uncle helped support us by paying the monthly mortgage. Naming my brother John was paying more dividends although I am sure my aunt had a lot to do with it. My grandmother, now retired, did not make much on Social Security but she helped us as much as she could anyway. She gave a little money and contributed by supplying some food. Since my mother would not go out, I had to do all of the shopping.

To help with the money I just had to go to work. My uncle gave me a job at his drugstore from after school until it closed. This was a seven day a week job as a soda jerk and delivering prescriptions. On weekends I worked only at night leaving time to play ball during the day. Although I did not make much per hour, I worked a lot of hours. The salary I made was small but it helped support our family. I claimed all the family members as my dependents on my income tax form. This prompted the IRS to audit me. I could still remember being asked how I could support so many on so little. I remember answering, "It ain't easy." Nevertheless, this rounded out our total support. At the time, I was only close to fifteen years old and could not drive yet. So I had the unenviable job of delivering the prescriptions on a bicycle. It was my cousin's girl's bike. This was hard work especially in the snow. There was not much time to study but I learned to do with less.

My regular playing days for the school were finished after one semester. My dream ended but our family had to eat.

We lived a very poor existence without a major bread winner in the family. The supermarket had ends of luncheon meats left after slicing with the machine. They sold them cheap rather than throw them out. To save money I bought these ends. That still stands out in my mind for two reasons. One because my mother did not shop at all. And second because I developed the ability to slice very thin. This came from holding these small ends then carefully slicing them as thin as possible to make the meat acceptable for sandwiches. This was quite a fete. As a result I became proficient at slicing all meats almost as thin as a slicing machine does. This was probably the only good thing that came of dad's escapade.

My father was rumored to be having an affair in Florida with a famous major popular celebrity singer. Eventually his money ran out and she dumped him. Could you imagine, when it was all gone, he had the gall to call, those he screwed to get help (money) to come back. Can you further imagine that they gave it to him. He first needed my mother's acceptance and then my uncle's money to return. My dumb aunt coerced my uncle into giving him the money. I really do not know what actually transpired between my aunt and uncle. But, in my mind, I could just hear my uncle shouting out "All right Hon, I'll give him the damn money. It's cheaper than paying the damned mortgage every month." My even dumber mother took him back. I could never understand why any woman would do such a thing. He came back under the ruse that he had to go away for his nerves. He was never nervous a day in his life as far as I could tell. But my dumb mom accepted it. Then to make matters worse when he came back she even slept with him. I do not know what he had but he hid it well.

My rebellious period seemed to end fast. It had a rather short lifetime. My teenage period was so short that I never really had one. I was becoming a grown-up early. I really never was a "teenager". Despite that, my sophomore year at school had been fun for me. Being on the baseball team gave me more friends in the student body. Most of the faculty seemed to like me as well. This made school a pleasure. It offset the pain of home life. Unlike my mom, I never accepted my dad's trip to Florida. To me it was not good to have my dad come home again. We managed fine without him, although my uncle might disagree.

Not long after his return home he quickly got into trouble again. Whatever he did required hiding from the police. He devised a unique hideout in his bedroom chest. The hideout was ingenious. My parents had a three drawer chest with two doors at the bottom. He removed the drawer bottoms so that he could enter through the bottom doors and hide in the empty chest. This hideout allowed him to not leave home. The police came to our house often but never found him. They searched the house several times with no luck. Who would ever open a drawer to look in a chest for him?

We also were instructed never to mention him or his hiding on the phone in case it was tapped. However the hiding meant that he could not go out to work. This was bad news for me. The outcome of this meant I had to continue to work to help support his family. My dreams of playing for the school were ended for good. That being the case I turned my attention to sandlot ball. I contented myself with playing ball on weekends. Despite these hardships, which never seemed like hardships to me, I breezed through my sophomore year without expending much energy. When the year ended I was surprised to see all B's on my report card. It amazed me to have done that well without even trying. I promised myself to put some effort into it for the next semester to try to qualify for college.

As it turned out I did not put all that much effort into it, but it was a little more than the year before. My effort was limited partially because my time was limited and partially because I lied to myself often when it came to certain kinds of effort. But my grades were good anyway. This I attributed to the very good memory with which I was blessed. It became obvious to me that if I listened closely in class I did not have to study much. As a result at the end of the semester my report card was all A's and one B in chemistry. Good as this report was, I knew the B was an undeserved mark. It should have been an A. My belief was that I knew more chemistry than my old lady teacher. Also I sensed she did not like me. It was probably my sarcastic mouth making trouble for me. The trait I had developed earlier as a cover-up for my shyness was now a habit that sometimes hurt me. Despite her blemish, my report card was certainly good. Most kids would turn cartwheels to get one like mine.

I still remember proudly bringing this report card to the car lot where my father worked. He was on the roof of the office shack. I held up the card to display it expecting praise. Instead he peered down and deflated me saying, "I see a B". There was just no pleasing this man. I sometimes wonder why I even tried. His words briefly hurt me but I recovered fast. Even if he did not appreciate it, I did. The last year and a half counted for college. Even though I did not study hard I felt ready to get those good marks.

During the summer I was playing baseball as usual. In one particular sandlot game I was having a good day at bat with five hits. I was playing centerfield that day. With a runner on first base the batter singled to centerfield. The runner tried to go from first base to third base. I made a strong, accurate clothes line throw to get the runner out at third base. It was a super throw befitting of a good major leaguer. After the inning ended a gentleman on the sideline called me over to him. He introduced himself as a bird dog scout for the New York Giants. He invited me to their tryouts in three days. The five hits did not interest him. It was the throw that caught his eye. Needless to say I was deliriously happy. A major league scout noticed me and would give me a tryout.

But my luck kept running bad because the very next day while horsing around with my friend, Mickey, I put my throwing arm through Mickey's back door window pane giving me a very bad cut. The result was fifteen stitches on the left wrist and no tryout for me. I consoled myself with the probability, almost certainty, that I would have never been selected anyway because of my lack of speed. From that day forward I spent most of my time at Mickey's house. We played many baseball and football board games together. I became very friendly with his entire family. It became like a second home to me. His older sister, Joyce, awakened feelings for girls in me. One of her favorite musical groups, The Four Aces, quickly became one of my favorites too. It still is to this day. But she was about twenty years old and too old for me. Because of our age difference I never expressed my feelings for her. Mickey's mom saw good things in me for the future. She prophesized I would have my name on my desk some day. Then Joyce got a boy friend and I slowly drifted away from their family. Later in life, when his mom's prophesy came true, we were no longer in contact with each other for her to realize she was right.

When school began in the fall I tried to ensure a good mark in gym to guarantee a place on the honor roll. Signing up for an automatic B for habitual honor roll students seemed the way to go to be certain. I liked Gym and really wanted to take it, but I was no gymnast and did not want to risk the honor roll when a sure B was available. I wanted to be assured of a B, so I waited in line to register. While standing in line with all the nerds that were habitually on the honor roll, the gym teacher spotted me. He had seen me play many times in gym and on the Jr, Varsity baseball team. He came over to me, took one look at my physique and said, "You will get your B but you're taking gym". That is all I wanted, in fact I preferred it that way. The gym class was first period every morning. A group of the boys, me included, in that class decided to come an hour early to play basketball. In those days I had lots of energy to burn. In spite of the early game every morning, I began to run to school to save bus money even though it was probably over a two mile run. I arrived at school every day an hour before the gym class began for our basketball game.

On the way to school, on most mornings, I had the good fortune of being intercepted by my math. teacher. That nice lady would always stop her car to give me a ride to school. During the many rides we got to know each other rather well. We grew to like each other a great deal. She was like another mother. She treated me like her son. After all I was her top student and a likeable kid. I could tell that the more she knew me the more she developed the feeling that I could do no wrong. In her normal testing of her students she regularly included an extra credit problem worth ten points. I finished every test correctly and got the extra credit too and always had time to spare. All my answers were always correct. I usually finished in half the allotted time. The course was solid geometry. As a result I had a grade point average of one hundred and ten. I was a whiz in that class and as I said always finished the tests quickly.

Often I finished so fast that I took the test for the girl I wished was my girl friend. Her name was Sandy. I hated to defy my friend, the teacher, but it was more important to me to make points with Sandy. To me she was beautiful. I wanted to take her out in the worst way. But I was too shy or chicken to even ask her. To impress her I did many math. tests for her. She would hand her paper down the aisle to me. On the way it passed through several girls. Then I took the test and passed it back. Everyone knew I liked her and the girls cooperated. Several times, when I had time, as a reward to the girls who helped, I even answered questions for them too. My math. teacher would never suspect me or even look my way. As a former teacher. it's hard for me to believe she did not see us. If she did, she never let it be known. She recognized that I knew the material as well as she did and either let us get away with it or never looked my way. After all, I was the apple of her eye. Needless to say I was popular with the girls for saving their rears. Unfortunately for me it was not the kind of like I was beginning to desire from girls. I was beginning to mature. But they all treated me sort of like a younger brother. I had not reached full puberty yet and they seemed to sense I was no threat to them. But I was beginning to gain on the maturity lost by skipping 3A.

The school year continued. As a combination jock-smart guy, I was well liked by most of the students including all the varsity players and especially by the girls that I helped. But as I said it was not the kind of like I desired from them. My hormones were finally beginning to flow causing me to recognize them as sexual beings. The feeling did not seem to be mutual. That was partly because I was so shy. I liked all of them but not like Sandy. She was far and away the No. 1 girl of my dreams.

The semester ended and again I had all A's and one B in chemistry. The old biddy did it to me again. But my revenge was coming. At that time a science organization requested that the school send several top science students for a test aimed at a scholarship to Harvard University. The old biddy did not select me. Fortunately, the head of the science department, who had formerly instructed me in Biology, overturned her ruling. He recognized me as a top science student and sent me too. When the testing phase of this venture was finished I had the top score from Lincoln High thus vindicating myself and showing the old biddy was wrong about me all along. Besides giving me an A in chemistry she should have picked me. It thrilled me to prove that she was wrong and must have had something against me. It turned out that I was the only Lincoln student selected for the next phase of the program, which was calling the students in for interviews. The grade the old biddy gave me lowered my grade point average undeservedly. She probably cost me a scholarship at graduation. But in retrospect I am glad. If I got it I would have never met my wonderful wife. Without her, I would not have my children and their children. Funny how things turn out in life.

The next step in the science organization's evaluation was to have small groups of interviewers see the many students from all over the city. So how well you fared in this phase depended a great deal on which group you faced. My group seemed to be looking for someone who lived and breathed science. That was not me at that time. My love and complete fascination with sports did not impress them. I knew what they wanted and could have lied but I could not be a phony. I stuck with the truth. My interview was doomed from the start. One drawback was that I was a very shy kid, not a conversationalist. Another was I had a poor vocabulary. Add to the mixture, my worldly knowledge and interests were limited to things in the sports world. Therefore I was not successful in the interview phase of the program. No scholarship was forthcoming for me. It was a shame because I doubted if my family would ever have the money to send me to college. I sure wanted to go. But as I said earlier, I was better off without it for the reasons mentioned previously.

The start of my senior year found everything the same at home. My father was still in hiding. None of my friends knew of this situation. Shame prevented me from telling anyone about it. I went out of my way to hide this thing that to me was so shameful. Even my best friends did not have a glimmer. This is what made school so much fun. I could get away from my miserable home life. My parents kept fighting.

My grandmother got involved on a night she was sleeping at our house. As I lay in bed the sounds of their fight were keeping me awake. My grandmother was yelling at her son to stop his shenanigans and get a job. I could not hear everything they were saying but she got so upset she ran up the stairs. I saw her go by my bedroom door in her nightgown. She was headed for my parents' room. There was really no reason for her to go to their room. Curiously I got up and followed her. Good thing I did. She went straight for the bedroom window. There was a chair in front of the window. She climbed on the chair and opened the window. Her body was half way out the second-story window preparing to jump when I grabbed her around the waist and pulled her back into the room. I probably saved her life or at least from serious injury because a cement patio was below. My dad had that effect on many of the female family members.

Another night my parents had a wicked fight. As usual I went to defend my mom. This particular time my dad got mad at me too. As the fight neared an end my dad gathered all my mother's clothes and threw them out the upstairs bedroom window onto the front lawn. He gave me the keys to the car and told us not to come back. This thrilled me. To me it meant she could finally get away from him. We gathered the clothes and put them in the car. Then we got in and drove away. As we drove away in the car she almost immediately began to waver. This was her usual reaction. He knew just how she would react.

The thought of finding her own place to live completely overwhelmed her. Her usual excuse for staying with him came quickly. She did not want to leave the kids alone with him. A request to take her back home came next. That would mean she was going to have to grovel to him. I tried to convince her otherwise by explaining that the last thing he wanted was to be saddled with the kids. He would give them back in a flash after he had a taste of caring for them. But he knew that she would not leave. She explained to me that he would hunt her down. Her words to me were, "He will find me wherever I go. You do not know your father." There was fear in both her voice and behavior. For the first time, I realized it was fear that bound her to him. The suspicion arose in my mind that she just wanted to be taken care of like a child. All these revelations made me realize that I was never going to save her from him.

School probably kept my sanity. Another memory from school is clear in my mind. One day in study hall the top boy in our class and I were talking. He was an all A student. The teacher/monitor came over to us and asked, "Why aren't you two studying?" We answered, "Everything is finished." Then she said, "Well do you have all A's?" "No we answered simultaneously, in one course we got a B." He and I were on the same wavelength. Then she ordered, "Well practice that." We looked at each other and said, "All right if you really want us to do it." Then we both got up and looked at each other thinking the same thing. Thinking alike we both began doing jumping jacks. All the kids in the study hall bust out laughing.

Not long after the big fight my mom announced she was pregnant again. I could not fathom how she could do it. She had to be a willing participant. I heard no fights or anything that even remotely sounded like a rape, so she must have been willing. In spite of all my dad had done to her and us she was with his child. How could she? That usually requires intimacy although it could have been fear or outright lust. Several times that year after big fights because of his bad behavior he faked suicide. One time she woke me up because he allegedly overdosed on aspirin in the bathroom and was vomiting. I pointed out to her that he would not hurt himself so it must be the Ipecac in the medicine chest. Another time he pretended to slit his wrists. The cuts were on the top of his palms not on the wrists. His explanation was, "I missed". No matter how lame his act was, she always fell for it. Many nights in my teen years I would hear them fight and dad dole out his usual abuse while I was in bed. I continued my vows that I would always treat my wife with love and respect and would have lots of time for any children.

The first semester of my senior year came to a close. Again I got all A's and one B. This time the B was in Physics and this time it was deserved. For some reason I did not grasp Physics as well as Math. or Chemistry. But as we got into the semester I got up the nerve to ask Sandy out on a date. She accepted and I was thrilled. I asked her to a dance so had to learn quickly. The box-step was quickly mastered but that was all I could do. We went on a double date to my friend's college fraternity dance. He was also backward around girls. He and I made a childish bet on who would kiss their date the most. We actually kept score. From his obvious actions Sandy figured out what we were doing. She deliberately started kissing me often including holding my face and kissing it. I could still hear him calling out "THEY'RE THROWING THE GAME". On the way home in the back seat of his car Sandy and I were kissing feverishly. It was a heavy petting session.

After we dropped her at her home my friend and his date warned me about her actions. They knew of my feelings for her and their intention was to spare me future heartache.

After she was gone his date said, "Girls don't act like that on their first date. Be careful with her." But you could not tell me anything bad about Sandy. To me she was everything good. At a later date I found out their suspicions were correct. Sandy previously went with a college boy. Then I talked to a friend from the football team who was currently dating her. According to him she was not a virgin even before he started dating her. There was at least one guy before him and he thought there were also some doctors at the hospital where she worked. One was a Puerto Rican so he dropped her. When I heard his story about her I was greatly saddened. It seemed she was probably a loose woman. At least I can thank her for one thing though. She taught me how to kiss a girl on that date. Unlike most boys my age, I was not looking for a loose girl. I wanted a girl with no sexual experience since I had none. I figured we could learn that together. The best thing that came from that date was that it unleashed me from my shyness with girls. I then started dating often. But I never mastered anything other than the box-step in dancing. The Jitterbug was out of the question for me. In my subsequent dates none of the girls kissed me like Sandy did. I only saw her one time a few years later. By then I was going steady with my future wife. Sandy no longer had that girlish look that she had in high school. We were only twenty. She looked a little haggard. Either she actually changed losing that cute young girlish look or I was blinded by love for my steady girl friend.

At the beginning of the next semester my mother gave birth to a baby boy. This was her fourth child and was the fourth time she had absolutely no say in the name. My father and grandmother schemed for a time then picked the name Albert after a rich uncle. Their hope was uncle Al would leave money to the kid in his will. My mother wanted the name Robert but had no say in the matter. After all she was only the mother. The timid soul did not know how to fight.

When Christmas time came the next year my dad came home dead drunk on Christmas Eve. He passed out on the couch. In the past he always waited until the Eve. to get a tree and toys. Then he would put it up for Santa to allegedly decorate it when he came with the toys. When all the decorations and toys were in place my parents would wake up the kids. Usually it was sometime after midnight. When the kids went to bed nothing would be there. When they came downstairs the sight of the tree and decorations would put them in a world of wonderment. I still remember it from when I was a child. It was so great that I later continued the tradition for my kids. This year would be different however. He came home dead drunk with no tree or toys then passed out on the sofa. So there would be no Santa or dad.

There was no way I was going to let the kids' Christmas be ruined that way. At that late hour I went out to buy a tree. The pickings were very slim. The tree vendor showed me how to make one good tree from two scrawny ones by drilling holes in one. Then cutting branches off the other. Next you sharpen the cut branches and jam them in the drilled holes. So I bought two scrawny trees and went home to make one nice one from them. When I finished it looked pretty good. After decorating it looked very good. Then I donated all my gifts as from Santa. The kids were not disappointed. We had a good Christmas and dad never awoke.

The next month graduation time rolled around. I was one proud kid. I was anxious to have my parents learn about my award and class standing. The final standings put me fifteenth in the class although many of those ahead of me were girls who took courses aimed at being nurses or secretaries. I finished as the fifth person in the Academic or college bound courses. In those days only boys did that. I also won the Mathematics Award. There was much to show my parents. Unfortunately the school was too new and only had four Academic Scholarships. That meant I did not get one. That was another disappointment in a growing list. Again in retrospect my life was better without one. Sandy and one of the other girls I took tests for got Nursing School Scholarships. So in some way I did help them. But the biggest disappointment came when I was sitting on the stage. I can still remember sitting there and scanning the audience only to find my mom sitting alone. Dad missed my third and most important graduation to date. Although I should have expected it, he crushed me again. The awards I won suddenly did not seem to mean as much to me. Another low hurdle was passed. It was not difficult but one that all kids wait for with great anticipation to begin their adult life. The next day he gave me a lame excuse why he was not there.

All through my senior year my father had been promising me tuition for college. Whenever I asked about it, his standard answer was "Don't worry about it, when the time comes I'll have it." That was his favorite answer but from past experience I knew he could not be trusted. I took the initiative and enrolled myself at Philadelphia College of Pharmacy and Science. I was going to be a Pharmacist. My uncle set an example and I was going to follow in his footsteps. I was even going to go to his Alma Mater. But when the time came to put up the money my father disappointed me once again. He was always disappointing me somehow. Like the times he got tickets for the Phillies World Series games and asked me to meet him there. Then he did not show up for the game. I sat all through the game alone. With his track record I should have known better by now. But in time it would prove he did me a favor by not sending me to pharmacy school. Because at the end I grew to dislike dealing with the public and I would have never met my wife. Wonderful Dad had now missed all three of my graduations and reneged on the promise of college tuition. I could have made the money myself but I had to support his family.

This was an important part of my development. I hated my family life and resented having to support his family. If he was stricken with illness I would gladly have done it. But I did not want to do it for his carousing. The experience did make me a better person. And later he tried to take credit for it. It maddened me, but he was correct.

CHAPTER 5

FINDING A FUTURE

Life was rather boring for me after high school. Occasional dates and playing baseball were the only things in my life that I enjoyed. The main problem was I hated my job. My aunt irritated me but the main reason was I could see no future in it for me. My future certainly did not look very bright at that time. My job was not an occupation befitting the fifth boy in his graduating class with the award for mathematics. College should have been in my future. But now, if some miracle got me in, I had no idea what to take as a major. Instead of going on to college I was still a soda jerk and delivery boy. The only consolation I had was that pharmacy was no longer in my future. There was good money in that field but I grew to hate the job.

My dad had unwittingly done me a favor by not coming through with the tuition money. My experience working with the public both in the store and delivering prescriptions made me hate dealing with the people. To me the people were cheap and completely unreasonable. They blamed me when drugs were expensive even though I only delivered them. The one good thing that improved my working conditions a great deal at the job was that I got a driver's license. This meant no more pedaling my ass all day. Still the only thing I liked about the job was working with my uncle. He was a nice person and I loved him. He made the job bearable. But despite the odds being against it, I still had college on my mind. Any major, in any school would be better than remaining as a soda jerk. Working at the drug store just because of my uncle dampened any hopes for a reasonable future. He was no reason to stay there and ruin my future.

On the other hand my Aunt Tootsie was in the store to deal with too. She was my father's sister. She completely cancelled out my uncle and then some. My aunt always found dirty work for me to do. She even made me care for her spoiled baby boy when he was having crying spells. He was too difficult for her to handle or she did not want to be bothered. So she pawned him off on me. I often had to take him upstairs to rock him to sleep. An example of other work I detested was dusting all the products on the store's shelves. The store was always very dusty for some reason. The dust just layered on all the product boxes.

Aunt Tootsie always waited too long to have it done. When it was very dusty then she made me do it. The other boy that worked there never seemed to get a chance at this job. That was probably because I was not allowed to say no. Dusting with a feather duster always raised enough dust to irritate my entire respiratory system. My bad allergy to dust would cause me to sneeze repeatedly. After dusting the store I would get all the symptoms of a bad respiratory cold. But did my aunt care. No. She gave me the job every time. To help a little with my problem I wore a handkerchief over my nose like a western bandit in cowboy movies. Any customer entering the store may have thought I was robbing it. But despite my suffering she made me do it. She showed no mercy.

My mother would get infuriated that my aunt made me do it causing me to get sick. But did mom do anything about it. No. She never even brought up the subject with my aunt. In the end mom always would say "we have to put up with it, she's doing us a favor." Mom was not putting up with anything. I was doing it. My aunt was not doing me any favor. Why should I have to put up with it. I could have gotten a decent job instead of remaining a soda jerk working for peanuts all my life. I just had to get out of that job and that's all there was to it.

Meantime at home things did not change much. Only my siblings were changing. My sister Molly, the terror, was growing into a ten year old tomboy. She would do things like hang upside down from tree limbs. She also protected our younger brother Johnny from a neighborhood boy who was bigger than both of them. The neighbor would bully Johnny. Molly would beat up the bigger boy. My brother Johnny was a cute, timid little boy. He was sort of like my mother. He always gave me the impression that he feared most things. On the other hand my sister was aggressive like my father. Both my siblings were growing up fast. Being so much older and working most of the time I did not see them very often, only at some meals, and on few nights. My schedule did not have much free time to do anything. They knew I was helping support them and seemed to look up to me as a protector or pseudo-father.

Things were still the same with dad. He kept pulling his antics on my mother and was either out of funds or hiding them from us. That meant I had to continue to contribute to the support of the family. I was almost as dumb as my mother. Now I realize things that were not apparent to me then. Dad was always short of cash and could not support the family. But somehow he managed to buy the used car business from his boss. Some Mafia type people seemed to be his partners. My dad was always associating with those types of people so it was hard to tell. He showed every indication he wanted to be a member of the "mob" if in fact he was not. Owning the business did ease our money problems somewhat but my parents still made me give my entire pay to the household. Again I just kept my tips. Fortunately for me, I made fairly good tips. That was mainly because I worked so many hours.

When I look back on it, I was a stupid kid to keep giving all my money. I was like the German soldier who just did as he was told. I like to think love of my family made me do it. But maybe it was some fear too. I just was raised to obey and never say no to my parents. Not only was I hurting my own future but I was enabling my dad to continue his escapades. My contribution helped him spend at bars and womanize. But what did I know, I was just a stupid kid who did as he was told.

Now my father owned a car lot. He offered me a gift probably to ease his conscience for the way he treated me. The gift was a 1937 Chevrolet 2 passenger coup with a rumble seat. It was sixteen years old. Only two years younger than me. My first inclination was not to take it. My feeling was I did not want anything from him. Then I quickly rethought the offer. My guess was that he would only sell the car and use the money for booze and women. So I took the car for my fun and to cut his funds. I was almost eighteen years old. Like any teenager I wanted a car badly. So I took the car feeling he owed me that much and more. When I got the car I made the mistake of placing the name of my current girl friend and me on the back using reflector tape. It read Jean and Lou.

Now that I had a car it was no longer necessary to run the two miles to work every day. I felt like I had it made. But my worries about a decent future were increasing. My worries about a career were known to my aunt and uncle. My aunt then devised a plan that would give me and her daughter a money making career. She approached me with her idea. Needless to say I was ready to jump at almost anything to be something other than a soda jerk. The career seemed to involve higher learning at a school. So I listened intently. The brother of her uncle by marriage had a successful Medical Laboratory. He was doing great financially. Her idea was for me to go to school to become a medical technician. Then in two years when her oldest daughter finished high school, she would also become a technician. Then my aunt and uncle would open a laboratory for us. My aunt predicted that their connections with doctors would lead to great success. I can see now that the idea was full of potential pitfalls. Knowing my aunt the Lab. would probably belong fully to my cousin, not me. She probably just wanted me to do all the work to get it started successfully. My guess is that then my cousin would walk in to a successful laboratory when she graduated and the it would probably belong to her. But, without thinking it through, I jumped at the chance to have a future and quit being a soda jerk. That week I registered at the Franklin School of Science and Arts. It was a two year accredited school for medical technicians.

Then two life defining events occurred in the same month that would affect my life forever. First a friend of mine wanted me to meet an Italian girl he knew. She was a customer at the local pharmacy where he worked. He arranged for me to meet her on her house patio in his presence. Her name was Teresa. She was a tall, very thin, good looking girl. Her looks were not movie star caliber but then neither were mine. She was not what I considered shapely and did not have great legs. Odd, because I was a leg man. Yet something about this girl attracted me. We hit it off immediately. After talking for a while, she accepted my offer for a date. Teresa was a real sweetheart of a girl. I shall call her Terri for the remainder of this book, which was her preference. I soon began to call her Tree since her mother always called her Treesa. That name stuck with me forever. Terri was only fifteen years old but had a lot of responsibility in her family as I did in mine. Our maturity levels seemed to match. Our first date came just as I started the Franklin school. It was a double date with the same friend as when I dated Sandy. We went to center city Philadelphia, which was a big deal in those days, to see the movie "From Here To Eternity".

My buddy and I played the part of big deals to impress the girls and sprung for a Taxi cab both to and from the theater. After the movie we thought it would be good to stop for some pizza on the way home. I knew Terri was expected home early and asked if she wanted to call her parents to ask if the added time was agreeable to them. When Terri came out of the phone booth she said her mother gave permission. The next day, I was told that I could not see her anymore. I found out her mom had said no to her on the phone. Her mom also did not like the way I kissed her good night. She was peeking out the window. Thus I began to learn Terri had a stiff backbone and a mind of her own. Later, I found out she had a fiery temper too. It was hard to imagine from this quiet, soft spoken sweetheart of a girl. Confronted with the prospect of never seeing her again, I took the blame and apologized to her mom for the lateness. I gave my word it would never happen again. This reinstated me.

On the way home in the cab I kissed Terri. This seemingly innocent event turned out to be just like a happening in a romance novel. A chemistry or feeling that till this day I call "MAGIC" flowed between us. At least I felt it. I did not know at the time if she felt it but I sure did. I just knew right then and there that I could not lose this girl. After that one date I felt sure she was the girl for me to marry if she would have me. The next day I opened a savings account to save my tips for an engagement ring. There was a problem now. I had a car with another girl's name on it. I tried everything but could not remove the tape. Terri said that she understood the situation and did not mind.

During the next couple of weeks I dated Terri each week. For the remainder of our courtship we went for walks every Tuesday evening and we kissed often. That magic was always there for me. I could tell it was there for her too. She may have been young but my feelings became cemented that she was the girl for me. I wanted to spend the rest of my life with her.

If she were not so young I would have asked her to marry me then. She was the first girl to kiss me with much more feeling than Sandy's. The chemistry was still there for me so I asked her to go steady. She accepted. Evidently she felt something special for me too. As I said, she was a tall skinny girl. I always teased her that if she did not wear a coat, I could not find her. She threw her lunch away every day at school to be thin. She practically starved herself since she always wanted to be able to see her ribs. As time passed, my feelings that she was the girl for me were reinforced further. It embarrassed me to have Jean plastered on the rear of my car. But Terri kept insisting that she understood. So every Tuesday evening we walked and kissed. I only drove when we were going to a distant movie. In a short time of continued dating I told Terri that we were going to get married if she would have me. This pronouncement took her by surprise. It sort of shocked her. After all she was only fifteen. But I was encouraged because she did not say no, just that I was crazy. In my mind this meant I had a chance. Now that marriage was on my mind I just had to find a better job until I finished school.

Then the second life defining event occurred. Luckily a high school friend came into the store to chat one day. I steered our chat toward me getting out of my nothing job. I told him my interest was in getting a real job. Hopefully I could find one with potential for a future. He mentioned that they were hiring youngsters for technicians at the Rohm and Haas Chemical Company. There was an aptitude test to be passed. He knew I was good in math. and science so he assumed that I would have a good chance. Their company laboratory location was not far away so I thought it was worth a try. That week I went to apply for a job. I passed the test with flying colors. I now had a decent job making more money. My work schedule now became five days at the chemical company and four nights at the drug store. Two nights were for school and one night was for dating Terri. Both my pays were entirely given to my parents. As before, I used my tips for entertainment and saving for an engagement ring.

My new job was a chemist's helper or technician in a polymer or plastic's science laboratory. As time progressed my boss and I built up a good relationship. It turned out that he was a member of that science committee that interviewed the high school students for scholarships to Harvard. He felt I had a flare for chemistry and was impressed with my knowledge at my young age and schooling level. He said, "They should have given you a scholarship. Most of those other kids should be butchers or bakers not scientists." He was continually urging me to drop being a medical technician and switch to chemistry. He emphasized the pay and prestige difference. I filed these comments away in my brain.

As time passed Terri's family became like my own. It got me away from the heartaches of my home. She had a nine-year old brother, Joe, who became like my own brother. He later became an ally against her parents. One night during our courtship Terri and I were in the kitchen of her house. As Terri passed me I grabbed her and put her on my lap. Just then her father walked into the room. He was an Italian gentleman from the old school and started cursing her in Italian. Italian was foreign to me so I did not understand a word he said. Later Terri told me what he said of her was not very nice.

I did not want her to take the heat for me grabbing her. So later I joined him in the living room and tried to apologize. He said, "Don't worry about it Louie, it's not your fault. The man is a hunter." I thought that's strange. He blames his daughter and not me. From then on I had to protect my girl friend. We needed a protective shield. I enlisted Joe's help. He got a quarter to watch out for their parents every time I kissed her.

From this start we began to build up a good older-younger brother relationship. A little later, he and my brother were on the same baseball team. Their team found themselves in need of a manager to start the season. There was no one to take the job. The kids really wanted to play so I took the job. I had to give up playing myself to take the coaching job. My schedule was tiring me anyway so I did not mind. Surprisingly, I found that teaching and being around the youngsters was more rewarding than playing. I liked the change. My baseball playing days had ended but playing football would continue. This cemented my relationship with Terri's brother, Joe.

Meantime Terri and I were becoming inseparable. Each of us now felt that we were meant for each other. More and more we felt like we belonged together and could not do without each other. These facts lasted all our lives. Our continual dates were leading to one conclusion. Marriage had to come soon because aside from needing each other so badly, I was going broke kissing her. There was no doubt she was a winner. All my friends and her friends liked her a great deal. In her high school yearbook they would call her a very sweet young girl. Although my mind was already made up, these facts convinced me further that my marriage decision was correct. Her kisses had already convinced me of that.

At work my boss kept encouraging me to change careers. Happenings at the school were beginning to convince me he was right. I was beginning to develop worries about the quality of the school and the students. The students were mostly from ghetto areas. Their education level was well below mine. As one example we were learning the Metric System in class one night. A girl was asked to change eighteen meters into millimeters. She gave some ungodly way-off answer. Then she said, "I know what I did wrong. I was supposed to multiply eighteen by a thousand and I multiplied a thousand by eighteen instead." I was in my chair at the time leaning back against the wall. I fell over at that explanation. This was the quality of many of the students in that institution. Meantime I was getting straight A's.

On the subway trip home I would occasionally see my teacher in the same car. As these ridiculous answers continued he came over to sit next to me one evening on the way home after class. The teacher said, "I am utterly disgusted with this class. Would you be willing to teach a couple of the classes to give me a break. If you would, I'll let you make up the final exam for the class. Then I will exempt you from it. I will give you an A on your report card." I was flattered and accepted the offer. My shyness made it difficult for me to teach the class but I overcame it. Later I thought more about this situation. I could not fathom going to a school that would allow me to teach and make the final exam. That coupled with my negative feelings about the career and my status as owner of the Lab. caused me to consider quitting Franklin. I talked it over with Terri. She was agreeable. So I quit Franklin. A little later my cousin told me she did not want to be a medical technician anyway. That was just her mother's fantasy. I now returned to not having a future but at least I had a decent job that I liked. As an added benefit I was making more money for my parents.

My continued serious feelings about marriage, more than ever put me in need of a more definite future. Franklin and any thoughts of a medical technical career were now behind me. I fully intended to marry Terri. She admitted the magic of our kisses flowed for her too. So she consented to the marriage. Now a career decision had to be made. I felt my future wife should be involved. So we discussed it at length. Her input was simple and to the point. She offered, "You have to do it, so it is your decision." Then the realization hit me that a career was not going to fall in my lap. I would have to get off my butt and decide on one all by myself. Since I was doing it, liked it and was apparently good at it, I decided on chemistry. To get started I had to cut my hours at the drug store and go to Temple University at night to be a chemist. My boss's continual prodding had finally convinced me to be a chemist. The most important thing was that I really liked it. It was a job I could see myself doing the rest of my life. It should pay a decent wage to raise a family with too.

Just as I was entering Temple night school, my boss and his entire group were transferred to the leather finishes laboratory. He was viewed as an up and coming young chemist in their organization. Leather finishes were how the company got it's start, so for some reason they put him there. Of course they had branched out into plastics with the discovery of Plexiglas and were now moving into fibers. The leather laboratory job was too mundane for my boss. It was a mistake to put him away from true science. Soon he left for a high ranking job at the Borden Chemical company.

Meantime I had a brand new job that was interesting at first. I learned to finish and refinish leather. I made trinkets for Terri. I even refinished her leather jacket. It was a professional job that essentially gave her a brand new jacket.

I also continually changed the color of her shoes to match her different outfits. The job was like taking arts and crafts. I tired of it rather quickly after the novelty of making items for Terri got old for me. I suffered from the same malady that my boss probably did. Chemistry did not seem to be involved at all. At first I wondered if I really wanted to be a chemist. But it seemed to me that the particular job is probably why my boss left. This laboratory was not helping my future. But I did not have the luxury of his Ph.D. I had to stay a while. I opted for a transfer to try my hand at analytical work after a year or so in the leather laboratory. This field definitely suited me much better than the other fields of chemistry. I was now sure that Chemistry was the career for me. Analytical chemistry was like trying to solve puzzles or do detective work. It was a perfect match for my interests. Besides liking it so much, I was good at it. In a short time I decided to be an analytical chemist.

At home my dad's continuing financial problems led him to take back the car he had given me. So he took back the first gift he ever gave me. This did end the embarrassment of the wrong girl's name on my car but it created a transportation problem for me to get to work and school. Without wheels I had to take two buses to and from work in the day and then two buses and the subway every school night. After working all day this got tiresome fast. So I bought my own car. It was a beat up 1947 Plymouth that cost me seventy five dollars at my dad's used car lot. I bought it from his partner.

Terri and I got engaged on Christmas of that year. It had taken me three years to save enough from my tips to buy the ring. We planned to get married September 1 of the next year, 1956. We decided to have an early autumn wedding so it would be cool. It could not be any later because of school. Terri would be eighteen and I would be twenty one. During our engagement we had a fight one night while on a double date. The reason escapes me but me trying to boss her around comes to mind. Well, nobody could boss Terri around. She threw the ring at me and said, "Marry somebody else." This gave me more of a glimpse at her temper. At first, I was not happy. Then after thinking it over a woman who would stand up for herself is what I wanted. Not a dishrag like my mother. That was the start of us becoming truly equals.

At the beginning of my second year at Temple night school I started to worry about how long I would have to endure this routine. It was work all day, go to school 2-3 nights a week plus study time. This routine would be necessary to get a bachelor's degree. I wondered how long so I mapped out the future to take a look ahead. It was revealing. Frankly, it scared me. When I laid out all the courses in their proper slots because of prerequisites, the result was illuminating. The bachelor degree would take me a staggering fourteen years in night school. This made me horrified. I could not tolerate that kind of schedule. I would be thirty-five years old when I finished if I was alive. The only good thing I could see about that is that I would be firmly entrenched in the company's pension plan by then. Of course, that would tie me to that company. But I might not want to be in that company at that time. This was an unacceptable situation to me. Just at that time I discovered the company was planning a new group within the Analytical division to work at night. Their purpose was to analyze pesticides on crops. I now got the idea to try to get into this group and switch to day school. Since marriage was now imminent this would be a big sacrifice for Terri. So we discussed it at length. She was agreeable with doing without me while I made this try. My acceptance into the new group would be my ticket to day school. I applied for the job. As a member of the division with a good record at work, I got the job. Now I could support my wife. It would be a massive undertaking to go to college full time in the day and work full time at night but in those days I thought I was superman. Besides, I would have preferred to work extra hard for three plus years rather than drag it out for fourteen years.

Now our time was spent planning a wedding. Anyone who has been through this knows how trying it can be. We were no exception. We did hit a snag planning our wedding reception right away. Terri's mom wanted a different kind of wedding than she did. I was so happy about just finally getting married to Terri that not having the kind of reception we wanted, did not bother me. It bothered Terri quite a bit. I guess it is different for girls. She wanted a sit down dinner with a limited number of family and friends. I really did not care as long as I got Terri. But her mother ruled. Her mom had the kind of reception she wanted. We had a buffet with lots of guests. Many of whom we did not even know. Terri could not budge her mom. I was afraid to say much. Terri was under age in Pennsylvania and we needed her mother's consent. I would not do anything to jeopardize getting Terri at this late date. To make matters worse I even had to pay for half of the wedding we did not want. My parents certainly were not going to pay any. Again, I would not do anything to risk losing Terri, so I paid but that bothered me. Also, it was ingrained in me never to fight with parents. But to help me out, my mother now let me keep my entire salaries. It was a good thing she did. Because, I also had to pay for clothes for the wedding for my mom and my siblings.

During the year I decided with agreement from Terri to take that night job and switch to full time day school right after our honeymoon. This would shorten the length of time until I graduated. In planning our future finances, we figured wedding gifts would help us with the tuition. The gifts actually paid for the first semester's tuition and a bedroom set. After those payments we had no money. For the second semester we would use the money from Rohm and Haas' plan. They paid half the tuition upon successful completion of the course with acceptable grades. Then we could make a loan from the neighborhood credit union to pay the other half. During the semester we could pay off the loan to the credit union. Then we could repeat this process every year. We knew that such a process would be necessary to reach our goal.

When our wedding time neared, it was almost ruined by my father. We planned a fountain of Manhattans as the only liquor at the wedding. My dad decided to buy liquor and bring it for him and his friends and only for them. This would be an ignorant gesture. Not to mention it would reflect on us. There would be none for my wife's family and our friends. I argued with him that this would be a rude and ignorant thing to do. I told him that Terri and I did not want it at all. There was no reasoning with him. Either I was not forceful enough or maybe he did not want his kid to tell him what to do. It seemed he would do it anyway. This raised Terri's Sicilian temper. Her stiff back and fiery temper began to show again. She stood up to him and told him emphatically that if he brings the liquor she would not be at the wedding. Dad had never been talked to like that by a woman. The way she acted is one of the things I always loved about her. She was always fearless. It was good to see dad beaten down, especially by a woman. My quiet and apparent calmness always seemed to me to be a good compliment to her outspokenness and fiery nature. Terri must have been convincing to dad about the wedding. I struck out when I tried. But he quickly dropped the idea completely when she threatened to not show up. It would appear that I was either not forceful enough or did not make the right threat.

By now Terri was 130 pounds up from her original 115. This was largely due to our Tuesday evening walks which always included a stop at a local grill for a corned beef on rye with French fries and a soda for each of us. I was happy at the weight gain because I thought she was too thin. Sort of like today's super models. Women like that do not please me.

Our wedding reception, while not to our taste, made most of the family happy. We picked Sept.1 so it would be cool. It was 99 degrees and 99% humidity. All through the wedding and the reception we were all dripping wet. After the reception I was driving one of my father's junkers to go home and change for the honeymoon. We took with us my sister and both our brothers. A couple of miles from the hall we had a tire blowout in a bad neighborhood. There we were stranded in a wedding gown and a tuxedo with three kids. Luckily a group of young boys saw how we were dressed and came to our rescue. They changed the tire and refused to take payment. We lucked out receiving such a nice gesture.

We then went home to get changed and embarked on our honeymoon in the Pocono Mountains. The picture taken by the photographer of us looking out of the back car window as we were about to leave shows how happy and in love we were. Like two senseless or stupid kids we never made reservations for that night. I should have known better. It was our plan to stop at a motel on the way there. Not only was it a weekend but it was Labor Day weekend. We had no reservations anywhere for that night. I stopped at every motel and hotel on the highway between Philly and Mt. Pocono with no luck. I even drove far out of the way in an attempt to find one. Failing to find a room we spent the night driving except for a stop to eat. Then we slept in the car when we reached the lodge in Mt. Pocono until our cabin was ready. That was some wedding night. This was the start of our life together. But the honeymoon was super wonderful. The two people that belonged together finally were joined.

We did have a marvelous time together during the week. There were many activities to make the week enjoyable. As long as we were together anything was going to be enjoyable. Like all good things the week came to an end and we left for home. On the way home the car again had a blowout. Luckily it was a back tire or my story may have ended there on the twisting mountain road. This was my third escape from death. My father did not have good tires for his car but he had a trunk full of them. So I changed the tire and we drove to begin our new life together. After we settled down from the honeymoon I began my tough schedule. I reserved Sundays to play football as a form of relaxing. But on my first week-end game my friend Mickey had his tongue split open. I looked down on his bleeding mouth. Realizing I had responsibility now and school to attend. I could no longer afford to be injured and lose time. I walked off the field and never played again,

Money was scarce as we expected. Even with both Terri and I working we still had to live with her parents which no newly married couple likes to do. And we had to pay rent. But in order to pay tuition and save for our own house it was necessary to live there. My old Plymouth was now gone. So Terri's father gave us his 1948 Dodge for me to go to work and school. This was a welcome help. As I said before our wedding gifts paid for a bedroom set and left just enough for my first tuition. But that is all we had to start our married life. We may have started our married life with zero money but we had each other and that was all that mattered to us.

When the semester ended the company paid half the tuition. We then borrowed the other half from the credit union for the next semester. As planned, we continued this process until school was finished. At the same time we saved for a house. This did not leave much money for any entertainment. That did not bother me much. I was usually too busy and tired anyway. But this did not make a fun life for Terri. I always promised her it would be better when we got older. That sweet girl never complained. She always said that I was doing it for our future and any kids we may have.

Our fiery love affair continued even though I was hardly ever home. Before we knew it Terri was pregnant. This happened when we decided to go au natural and have a baby whenever it happened. It happened that night. Preparing for the baby then actually having it, slowed our savings a great deal. This prolonged our stay at my in-laws home. The school year went well. I got A's and B's in my science, Math. and German courses. They were the only ones that mattered to me. I got C's in the liberal arts courses which did not matter near as much. My time was limited and I decided to devote more of it to the subjects important to my career.

My schedule was boring to me as well as to Terri. She now had to quit work to have the baby. This slowed our savings even more. Terri had a difficult time with the delivery but produced a baby boy. She developed toxemia at the very end which raised her blood pressure rather high. As all parents know, there is nothing like the miracle of birth. When I saw him, it was difficult to believe he was ours but there was no mistaking the Papa lip. I had a bald uncle and he looked just like him. Terri insisted on naming him Louis after me but I did not want him to be a Junior. So, we inserted a C for Christopher as his middle initial. He was born on Columbus day. As a slap at my father we defied the old Italian tradition of naming a son after the paternal grandfather.

Baby Louis was a real joy to us. Like all new parents we went overboard on having pictures taken. We could not really afford them but did it anyway. All our parents really enjoyed him too. There was a special significance to the joy he brought to my father-in-law. Pop was going through the process of being swindled out of his business. Playing nightly with baby Louis helped grand pop survive these difficulties. Playing with the baby every night would relieve him of his depression and may have avoided a nervous breakdown.

After about a year and a half of continual use for school and work the '48 Dodge died. We had to junk it leaving me with no transportation again. After taking buses and the subway for about a month my father came through with the second gift he ever gave me. It was a 1949 Chevrolet. My father-in-law's previous gift of a car probably made him feel guilty. Whatever the actual reason I now had much needed transportation.

As if we did not have enough problems, the baby now got sick to the point where he could hardly breathe. His Pediatrician placed him in the hospital. As part of the treatment Louis was put in an oxygen tent. Louis got pneumonia before the illness ran its course. Eventually he got better. This worry is just what we needed while I was struggling through school. Shortly after he got better, Terri began to want another baby so Louis would have a playmate. She did not want him to grow up alone. It did not take long and Terri was pregnant again. Now we had to move because of lack of room. My salary had slowly advanced so we thought we could afford the payments on a small row house. I found a small two-bedroom row house on would you believe it Terry Street. Terri did not believe me when I told her. It was a small house but at a price we could afford.

Just about that time baby Louis got his second episode of not breathing well. We went through the same process as we did previously. He went to the hospital wound up in an oxygen tent. Again he wound up with pneumonia. We had this worry as we moved in the new house in July 1958 while I was attending summer school. That year I attended summer school in our first months in the new house for the expressed purpose of graduating next June for a total of three years plus 3 night classes.

The cost of the new house was difficult for us but worth the chance to be alone. As an example of our financial situation I had taken my dad to the settlement for the house. It turned out that I was seven dollars short. He gave me the money to complete the sale. That was the third gift from my dad. My schedule was a real drudgery to me and to Terri. I hated it. Every day when I left school I would stop at the car and wave back at the school saying that is one more day I do not have to come back. But I knew the end was near. Moving into our own house meant Terri no longer had use of her mother's clothes washer and drier. Her grandfather donated his almost new wringer washer. Terri would have to wash the clothes then run them through the wringer to remove the soapy water. The next step was to replace the wash water with rinse water and rinse them. Then she would run them through the wringer again to remove the rinse water. Finally, she would hang them out to dry. She struggled through this with a large pregnant belly. During the struggle she would get very wet. When I saw her do it, I went out and bought her an automatic washer and drier on time.

Despite those feelings I began to consider going to graduate school for a Ph.D. degree. It was in my mind at the time of the house purchase. I never should have purchased a home if I thought it through. But the field of chemistry had changed to the point that the advanced degree was like a union card. The bachelor's degree was becoming like a technician. I wanted desperately to make a nice life for Terri and any children we may have so they would not have to struggle like I did. This thought spurred me on as my schedule was getting harder on me. But I wanted to protect my investment of hard work.

In late March Terri gave birth to another baby boy. We named him Michael. This delivery was even more difficult for her than the first. She developed a more severe case of toxemia with higher blood pressure than with the first child. She barely survived this time. She also gained a good deal of weight which was difficult for her to lose. We then considered having no more children. It seemed detrimental to her health. Now that we had two children, my thirst to get a higher degree was quenched quite a bit.

Michael was another bundle of joy. There were not a lot of pictures this time because we had even less money than the first time. We now had a mortgage to pay and Terri no longer had a paying job. A rather unique episode in Michael's first few months of life comes to mind. Early on Michael was acting like he was not getting enough food. We finally traced this to Louis stealing his bottle. The bandit would steal his bottle, drink it and then was smart enough to put it back. That is why it took us so long to discover the caper. It was difficult to get angry with Louis. First of all he was so cute. And secondly, he got another attack of bad breathing ending in the hospital with another case of pneumonia.

Now that we were in our own house we would periodically get a call late at night from my brother Johnny. The abuse dad was giving mom was scaring him. We would have to go over and calm things down. Several times we took my mom and her kids to live at our house until dad came to his senses and settled things. Despite these problems graduation rolled around and I had cleared my highest hurdle so far. To me I thought there could never be one higher. That is how taxing it was on me.

I sat at the graduation ceremony thinking about all the hard work I had finished. I was proud of myself. Attending college full time with a full time job is a difficult accomplishment in itself. To do this with a two children family makes it an all the more admirable achievement. But I had done it. I felt like it almost killed me but I had done it. But I could have never done it without Terri. Besides being a good wife and mother, she was my lover, soul mate and best friend. I became glued to this young woman. We were joined at the hip so to speak. A couple of my friends were on the same schedule as I was. They were single and quit the drudgery short of their degree. They had no Terri to aid and comfort them. Whenever the going got tough and I was ready to quit, she was there to pick me up and inspire me. After her magic I always continued. Just her touch gave me a warm and calming feeling. She told me my touch did the same to her. Touch was an important thing to us. We could recognize each other's touch. In fact, we won a contest at a party as the only couple who could recognize each other's touch while being blindfolded.

To me it was a happy graduation ceremony. For both of us it was a happy moment. To me it meant my drudgery was complete. We both had accomplished this degree together. Few people knew just how hard it was on me or her. Only my wife, who saw me passed out on the floor one morning from studying German all night for a final exam, knew what I really went through. Another morning she had to drive with me to school to keep me awake after two consecutive nights of not sleeping to study for a physics final. I got an A in that final which I needed for a B in the course. I was so tired and in a near trance that the knowledge must have just flowed out of me.

For the fourth time my father was not at my graduation. Even a college ceremony did not attract him. It did not bother me so much this time because I was accustomed to it by now. But the real reason was I had my Terri with me. Seeing her in the stands made it all worth while. This had been drudgery for her too. She was alone most of the time raising the two boys. She essentially had no husband and had to do almost everything herself. I cherished this accomplishment mostly because I could share it with her. It truly partly belonged to her too.

Now that I was making a little more money we decided to buy a present for my bother Johnny. He was a fanatic about the clarinet. He used the wooden leg of a small table as a pretend instrument. All day he would place the leg to his mouth and imitate all the gyrations of the jazz clarinetists. Terri and I never saw anybody so in love with an instrument. So we decided to indulge him. We scraped together the money to buy him a clarinet, a book to learn how to play and some sheet music. We never saw a young boy so happy. In an extremely short time he knew how to play and could play every song on the sheets. Terri and I were happy and felt we had done a good thing.

During that year two things happened to influence my decision about going for the higher degree. I worked in a laboratory that analyzed and developed methods to analyze pesticides on crops. My boss assigned me to develop a method to determine a new pesticide on crops. I developed a plan and showed it to him. In response he bet me a steak dinner it would not work. When it did work, I wrote up a method and left it on his desk expecting a dinner. There was never any dinner. Then, to my horror, I saw my developed method typed with his name on it instead of mine. In analytical chemistry there is no greater crime than stealing another chemist's method. He downright cheated me and took the credit. This would undoubtedly affect our raises. I was incensed. My hard to arouse temper was now aroused. It overcame my shyness. We had words over this piracy. I told him I was going to get a Ph.D. then come back and fire him.

The second thing that happened was a Temple graduate in my class was hired at a higher salary than I was making. I went to our personnel man for an explanation. He said it was because my length of service allowed me to collect pension money. When you add the pension to my salary our salaries are comparable. This is not true. The other man will start drawing pension money from a higher salary. His salary will increase from a higher starting point. I will never catch him. They obviously did not recognize and reward talent. My boss stealing my method may have played a role in this. I decided then and there not to work for them in the future. So I would never return to fire my boss.

That night I talked to Terri about the situation. I voiced my concerns about wanting to go but not letting her and the boys live like paupers. My ever understanding wife said they would be fine. I should follow my dreams. I then made up a primary list of schools based on the professors there and their notoriety. Armed with this list I immediately wrote to them. Iowa State, Michigan, Kansas and North Carolina were on my first list. My laboratory head had given me the name of a great up and coming young professor. He was Charles N. Reilley at the University of North Carolina (UNC). For this reason he was included in my first list of Professors that interested me. The other schools I picked myself based on type of research the Professors were doing. All of the schools to which I applied accepted me. They all made me essentially the same offer. I would be a teaching assistant, which means teach laboratory classes and otherwise aid the professor. For this I got a lowered tuition which was about equal at each school with a salary of two hundred dollars a month. Our decision seemed difficult at first.

Then the head of the department at UNC called my wife. He was from Philadelphia too and promised us cheap housing which was difficult to get. This personalized call helped sway us to UNC. Then Reilley's reputation and flexibility for Thesis choice added to it. Then we considered other factors like the closeness to home, a big item was the lower cost of living, the better weather conditions which meant lower heating bills. The choice became clear. I chose UNC and never got a chance to make a second list. The money was still not enough to live on so we made a government loan which we renewed every year we were in school.

CHAPTER 6

HEADING SOUTH

Now I had made a really tough decision. The school and more importantly the professor for whom I was to do my graduate work were selected. That is very important when you try for a job. Your potential employer counts that a great deal. But time was running out on me to get ready for the move. It was almost too late now. Like most of our life this would be an occasion when Terri and I, do to our own making, were rushed. It was mainly my fault for waiting so long to decide if and where to go. At any rate we had many important things to accomplish before we could leave. There was not much time to accomplish them. We had to move fast to make all the necessary arrangements to prepare for our move. First we had to select an agent to handle renting our house. We hoped the rental could be accomplished rapidly. Our finances could not take much of a delay paying the mortgage without a renter. We could only last one month. Next we had to find and hire a mover to take our belongings to North Carolina. The last item on our list was to plan how we would get there. Taking things in order of importance we first contracted a real estate agent to get them moving on the house rental. Next we arranged for a moving company to haul our household belongings.

The last item seemed the simplest on the surface since we only had to address getting there. The first thought was all we had to do was buy a map. But it was not that simple. My Chevy had seen better days. I did not trust the car for the five hundred plus mile trip south. So we really had a problem without funds to buy another car. Our luck was not all bad. Luckily at that time the man next door to us was selling his '49 Mercury. The asking price was cheap enough, only $250. The car seemed like a good running vehicle. It seemed perfect for our needs. The only problem was we could not scrape up the two hundred and fifty dollars necessary to buy it. A co-worker heard of our plight and came to our rescue. He was good enough to offer to lend me the money to purchase the car until I got my money that had accumulated in my pension fund at the company. He offered the loan without my even asking. No other person offered to lend me the money. Not even any of our family members offered. When I purchased the car, the Chevy was given back to my dad. To my way of thinking the proceeds from any sale should belong to him. That would make me not feel indebted to him. That was important to me. I did this even though I assumed he would use the money for his no good deeds.

Now that I was going to have a much lower paying job, I had to drop my life insurance. Leaving my job meant no medical insurance for the family either. Thus we were going to risk living with no insurances at all. Although as a student I had free use of the University Hospital and did not know that yet. We believed the family would have no medical coverage. I would not take that risk today. But we were young. Being without these insurances did not worry us at first. We had not thought this out and planned ahead. Just like not getting motel reservations on our wedding night. This episode burned a lesson in my brain. From then on planning ahead became a way of life to me. Sure enough, as the time to move approached, Terri and I began to worry. We also worried about the quality of medical care for the boys once we arrived. This was our main concern since our son Louis was hospitalized periodically.

We never thought of this medical situation with all the excitement of quitting work and picking a school. Terri was already worried but now so was I. I was a person who never worries. But now even I was beginning to worry. At this late date I decided to check on the availability of a good hospital for the boys. I also wanted to know if there was any medical coverage issued by the school for the family. A phone call to the school quelled my fears. Sources at the university answered both questions assuring me not to worry. They informed me that UNC had an excellent teaching hospital. Along with nearby Duke University they were reported to be the best hospitals in the state and among the best in the country. They further informed me that as a student, my entire family was completely covered at the UNC hospital. This took a large weight off our minds. It appeared we had no worries about our children or major medical expenses. We lucked out on that. Then both of us decided to chance my survival and do without the life insurance.

Terri kept an immaculately clean home. To outsiders it was always considered in move-in condition. This made the real estate agent's job easy. The agent found renters for the house very quickly. The first prospects took it. Thus the impending financial burden was removed. The renters would take over the house just two days after we left. Things were working out nicely. All the necessary items were now settled so we could plan our trip to Chapel Hill. Terri's parents and her brother Joe would go along with us. They would be driven by her mom's cousin who would take his wife along too. The cousin was an experienced driver with many driving trips to Florida under his belt. Our escorts would follow us in her cousin's car. Our plan was to travel at night to avoid traffic. We decided to put a padded plywood board in the back of our car so the children could sleep comfortably on the way down. Before we left the company paid me my accumulated pension money.

Then I immediately paid back the loan to my friend. The moving men came on time and took our belongings. After saying good-bye to all our neighborhood friends we were ready to embark on our adventure.

Before leaving, my wife and I went to say good-bye to my parents. My mother acted very scared that I would give up my job to attempt this venture. She was always afraid of any major life change especially if it involved risk. She behaved in a similar manner when I quit Franklin to be a chemist. She uttered exactly the same words as she did then, "Are you sure you know what you're doing?" Her tone was of fear and disapproval. My mom was not a daring or venturesome person. My dad on the other hand was that kind of person. But he outwardly took an even more negative approach than she did. He tried to talk me out of going. He acted like I was crazy to even consider it. His argument was that I was a chemist with a good paying job and was doing well at my job. Why give it all up for a "maybe"? His memorable quote was "do you go to school to get dumber". My dad had no understanding of working hard to better oneself. In fact, I think he had no understanding of working hard, period. It was my guess that he influenced my mom to be so negative.

We joined the others to begin our bold adventure. When we crossed the Delaware Memorial to leave New Jersey the trip began to get harrowing. There was a terrible fog that night over most of the Atlantic coast states. The fog arrived just as we entered Delaware. My experience driving on the highway was very limited. It was also rare that I drove on a highway at night. This would be my first experience in fog too. The combination was wicked for me. The conditions we faced seemed to me to be bad even for an experienced driver. They were really nerve racking for me. Frankly, I was scared for my entire family. We were traveling on a two lane highway and I was driving rather slowly. I was so tense gripping the wheel that the muscles in my back and neck ached. My driving must have clogged traffic because there was a rather long line of traffic behind me. Most of the other cars were passing me. Some were honking their horns. Apparently experienced drivers could handle it. They probably cursed me as they passed. But I could not see well at all because of the headlight glare on the fog. I thought the other drivers were crazy to drive so fast in these conditions. My wife and kids were in the car so caution was my main concern. To me driving slowly to be safe was a necessity. Then to add to the driving difficulties, our oldest boy vomited all over the back section of the car.

We had to pull the car off to the side of the road in the heavy fog. This seemed a bit hazardous to get out of the car and be exposed to the traffic zipping by us. Despite this, I welcomed the change from the tension of driving. We thoroughly cleaned up the mess in those dangerous conditions. This further lengthened the time of the trip. In the early morning we were about two thirds of the way through Virginia when either we came out of the fog or it lifted. Whatever the case it was gone. My wife and I cheered. Suddenly my fear vanished and the muscles in my back and neck relaxed.

This seemed a good time for a rest room stop so we could stretch our muscles, go to the restroom, relax and eat breakfast. After the stop the remainder of the trip was pleasant. We made our way to UNC. We had to go to the student housing called Victory Village. As we drove through Chapel Hill it was reminiscent of the southern towns I had seen in many movies. Finally we stopped at a gas station to get directions to the village. Then we made our way to the rental office of our new residence.

The people at the office took our first month's rent then gave us directions to our house. Driving through the village revealed it's unique nature. The housing was like a project. Later we found out it was cheaply built for the G. I.'s returning from World War II. At this late date it was still standing. The homes were built from some sort of cardboard-like composition board. You could bang a hole through the outside walls with a hammer. This would be our home for the next three to four years. We drove down the winding streets of the village looking for our new house.

In a short time we found our little single house at 180 Daniels Road. We entered the home wondering what the next few years had in store for us. In a short time the movers arrived with our belongings. They arrived within an hour of that promised. Things were going well. We were off to a good start. That ended quickly. As the women were putting the dishes away to straighten out our kitchen they were greeted by roaches. It was a different creature than those back home, but still a roach. This gave me, and I am sure, Terri a sick feeling in the stomach. Did I bring my family to live like this? I asked Terri if she wanted to go back home right now. Telling her I would understand. I knew how bugs, especially roaches, bothered her. But my ever loving Terri thought of my career dream and opted to stay. These roaches were not like the critters back home. They were smaller, long and thin and were brownish in color. We would later find out they were called German roaches. They generally come into your home with potatoes. Later we discovered every one of those cardboard houses was infested with them.

After we settled in the house we got a good night of sleep. Our five companions got their sleep at a nearby roach- free motel. And so our life in Chapel Hill began.

CHAPTER 7

LIFE IN CHAPEL HILL

First thing the next morning we had a bout with the roaches. After that I went to the Chemistry office to report my arrival. The first order of business was introductions to the entire office staff. Then the head of the department informed me that all new graduate students had to take exams. They were called proficiency exams. It just thrilled me to hear that. There were four exams in the four fields of chemistry. The purpose of the exams was two-fold. Most importantly the school had to be sure you were competent to teach your assigned course. The other purpose was to uncover any courses in which you may be weak. Then you could repeat any such course until you got a B. The exams were scheduled in just four days. My weakness in Inorganic and Physical chemistry would require me to study further. My expectations were as follows: I was good in Analytical chemistry, my anticipated major field and excellent in Organic chemistry, my expected minor. There was no need for me to study these latter two subjects. My study time was spent on Physical and Inorganic Chemistry.

When the results of the tests were recorded I failed the Physical exam, just barely passed the Inorganic, did well in Analytical, and excellent in the Organic test. Because of the failure I had to repeat undergraduate Physical Chemistry. On the other hand I was assigned to teach Organic Chemistry. The Organic test was a breeze for me. I was sure of a super grade. That was my favorite subject course wise I was good at it and did very well. At Temple I got an A in both the Organic and advanced Organic courses. I was very interested in it. After all our bodies are organic chemical factories. So, I had a keen interest in the subject matter. But I had no interest at all in the things organic chemists do in the laboratory. My high results caused all the Organic professors to try to persuade me to switch major fields. Their obvious hope was I would then select them as my major professor. But I liked Analytical Chemistry. It fit better with my likes and abilities. It was a problem solving field. First of all I have a strong interest in problem solving. Secondly my feelings were that most of things in the world, including all people, are made up of organic chemicals. Therefore my knowledge and love of the organic field would not go to waste. In fact, it would be a great aid in developing methods of analysis. As an example, the pesticide for which I developed a method at my former job was an organic chemical as are most industrial pesticides. My knowledge of Organic Chemistry was very helpful in that development. My boss' inferior knowledge probably caused him to say it would not work.

When I got home from school that day, Terri had planned a defense against the roaches. She insisted I spray often. This I was sure would not work. When I sprayed them, the roaches seemed dazed by the spray. I would throw the apparently dead critters in the trash can but they would only climb out later. So we decided to put much of our food in the refrigerator and tape shut all opened box food. We kept our dishes standing in the drying rack on the sink so roaches could not contact them. This would be our initial defense and we could add things as we thought of them. Our minds were taken off the roaches by a call from my brother John. He had his usual tale about mom and dad. I told him there was nothing I could do at this distance. He should not call anymore except to say hello or give news. This repeated scenario had me and I'm sure Terri damned tired of it. But I knew how he felt. I went through it and I was not the timid type.

When I got back in the swing of school the Organic professors exerted a mild pressure on me to switch fields. Despite this my love of developing methods of analysis caused me to select Professor Reilley and Analytical Chemistry as my major field as I had initially planned. Professor Reilley assured me I could work on anything remotely related to analytical for my thesis. He even offered me the synthesis of indicator dyes used in analysis. I felt this was really an Organic type thesis. He was offering me that to possibly appease my interest in Organic Chemistry. But I liked the subject matter of Organic Chemistry not the laboratory work those chemists perform. Otherwise I would have majored in organic. Those chemists cook up smelly chemicals all day in glass vessels to synthesize new chemicals like cooks in a kitchen. I like cooking but only if it tastes and smells good. The things Analytical Chemists do is what interested me. But suddenly I felt important. It made me feel important to have professors trying to lure me into their groups. But the important people of the department, probably because of my grade, decided that I would be a graduate assistant in Organic Chemistry. Despite the fact I had decided to stick to my first love and major in Analytical Chemistry.

Graduate school was long hours of study and research. The teaching staff was amiable as were the students. Occasionally we would all get together for a game of touch football. That would relieve the tensions of going to school. The faculty and graduate students developed as close a relationship as those positions would allow. My schedule did not allow me to be at home very often. But the schedule was much easier on me than it was in undergraduate school with a full time job. But difficult as it was for me, I, at least, was with adults all day and could talk with them. Poor Terri was stuck alone in a foreign land with two young children who could not carry on a conversation. During the second month at our new home we were feeling lonely and missing home. This led to needing each other badly and Terri got pregnant again.

The stay in Chapel Hill, probably aided by the pregnancy, began to get to Terri rather quickly. She had a very lonesome life. Not only was she alone with the kids all the time but the attitude of the native townspeople in general and the store clerks in particular began to irritate both of us. It bothered Terri more than me. They all talked with thick southern accents. Then they acted like they did not understand us. Their attitude was like we did know how to talk. They always implied we could not speak well. This bothered us, especially Terri, because we knew damn well they understood us just fine. Finally Terri's Sicilian temper exploded once again. She turned on a TV in the store then told the clerk you understand the people on TV just fine. Well those people talk like we do, not like you. The clerk was stopped in his tracks. To add to this kind of treatment, while hanging clothes one day she overheard neighbors saying "THE YANKEES OUGHT TO GO HOME." This treatment got to my young, pregnant, lonely wife.

Similar treatment was doled out to me by the students at school but being the teacher I had the power seat. One day I was writing on the board with my back to the class. I was able to write with either hand because my early teachers would always pull the pencil out of my left hand and place it in the right one. Their insistence completely converted me. So being able to write with either hand I tried to impress the class. I began to write a sentence with my left hand starting at my left. Then when I reached my body, I switched the chalk to my right hand and finished the sentence to the right. A disguised voice squealed out from the back of room "HSSST GO HOME YANKEE." Not easily agitated and having a quick sarcastic mouth I answered without turning around, "Shut up or we'll beat you again." I never got any lip again. Even though in general this was our typical relationship with North Carolinians, I became good friends with this class. That was probably because I gave them special tutoring classes on my own time.

But the southerner's general attitude made life much harder on Terri than me. At school the graduate students and faculty were almost all from out of state. So they did not have the prejudice toward northerners. The home state students had to deal with me in a power position and could not show their bias. But Terri did not have that advantage.

The ever present roaches began to bother us but especially Terri. One day a neighbor friend came in and I swallowed my pride and told him about them asking if he had any. He answered, "Brown ones about this big?" He held up his hand with the thumb and index finger apart by the approximate size of a roach.

I replied, "Yes."

He continued, "When I left the house there were two columns of them crossing the living room floor."

That answer indicated to me that we had to learn to live with them like all the other people do. I went out and bought a dart gun with the suction cups on the end. From then on I used the roaches as targets when they were climbing up the walls. Soon I got very accustomed to them. When I would study at night my body would be still for a long period of time. Then the roaches would slowly crawl up my back. I would just flick them off the back of my neck. Terri could never get that accustomed to them. It was partially a mother's concern for her children. She thought both of my practices, the flicking and the darts, were gross. I just always learned to adapt to the situation. Some were too gross for her.

Teaching was a new and generally pleasant experience for me. At first I sort of fell in love with it. I thought of becoming a college professor. Then I considered the difference in initial salary compared to an industrial position and wavered. The clinching reason was in order to be a successful research oriented university professor in chemistry required long hours away from your family. This did not interest me and ended any thoughts of teaching.

Many things were memorable in my first year teaching. Two events that occurred stand out in my mind. An attractive young girl approached me needing an "A" in laboratory to get into Medical School. Her words were "I would give anything for an A." She knew I had a pregnant wife at home and I guess thought she would try her luck. I was not flattered that she asked because of her motive and because I was in love with Terri. Since I had no interest in playing around with her, my wise-cracking mouth asked for fifty thousand dollars. Remember this was 1960. She said. "Are you crazy?" My answer to this was, "If I get you into Medical School now, you will have one more year of practice before you retire. You will probably make $100,000. that year. I want half. In retrospect due to inflation I should have asked for more because that hundred thousand is like a million now.

The other event came when I was marking laboratory notebooks. I caught three identical books because they all used the German word mit in their write-up. That alerted me to it. Then a careful inspection revealed that all three write-ups were word for word the same. So I graded the experiment write up as a 99. Then I divided by three and gave them each a 33. One of the students was my neighbor. When he complained the penalty was too severe. I explained the school was on the honor system and as an alternative I could have had them expelled.

Baby Louis got another episode of his poor breathing during that first semester. The baby next door to my mom had recently died from a breathing problem before his parents could get him to a hospital. So I frantically rushed him to the hospital. The doctors took him in a room and returned with him in about twenty minutes. They said he's well now you can take him home. I asked, "Aren't you going to put him in an oxygen tent?" The Doctor answered, "No, if we do that he'll just get pneumonia. Just give him this Benadryl for allergy and if he has trouble breathing go in the bathroom and run the shower real hot. The humidity will clear up his congestion fast." How revealing. The treatment in Philly was giving him pneumonia. The trip to graduate school was worth it just for this discovery. In all future events, this treatment worked.

The year marched ahead with us finding it difficult to live on so little money. But it was a good thing we chose UNC. The cost of living was much cheaper. The food, heat and rent were a good deal cheaper there than at home and at the other schools. We also found it a lonely and boring life. Terri seemed to be headed for a nervous breakdown so we flew home for thanksgiving to give her a break. Terri and the kids remained with her parents. I returned to school alone. It was my first time without Terri since we got married. Now I was lonely but had school to occupy me. Still, I could not wait till Christmas vacation to rejoin her and take a break till New Year day. Our stay at home was the highlight of the year. We were glad to be home together and see all of our family members. That coupled with the break from studies made it quite enjoyable for me. It was especially enjoyable to be around our kind of people. Graduate school was easier on me than my time at Temple. I did not have a full time job there. Thus I did not mind going back. But I hated to return to those roaches and living conditions in general. I hated it as much as Terri did but did not let it bother me as much as she did. We had an on-going battle with the roaches. I refused to let it get to me. Persistent calls to the exterminator did no good. I sprayed so much the family's exposure surpassed that of the roaches. I would spray in the kitchen and they would go through the wall into the bathroom. Then I would run around to the bathroom to spray. They would go back through the wall into the kitchen. This cycle was repeatable. It was like a game. As a chemist I knew the spray was going to get us before it got them. So I quit.

Meantime back in school the time had come to begin to think about the language requirements. It was required to pass exams in German and another language of my choosing for my degree. German was required because most of the early chemical literature was in that language. I expected no problem having passed three years of German with all B's at Temple. The second language figured to be a problem. I never had any second language. My friends all said French was easy so I made it my second choice. When the time came a one year course might be enough to pass it.

The first semester of school ended with me in position to pass everything except for possible trouble in Inorganic Chemistry. During the second semester I took the German exam. I thought it was a snap especially since they allowed the student to use a dictionary. But to my surprise they failed me. A professor showed me the exam. There was only one mistake on an entire page of translation. His explanation was that I translated a singular as a plural which showed no understanding of the language. In my opinion this was downright robbery. I was furious. But he was the boss. My only consolation was that I could take it as many times as necessary.

When the second semester ended I had passed the undergraduate physical chemistry course to complete all my proficiency requirements. Unfortunately I got a C in my Inorganic Chemistry course which in the UNC graduate school is a non-passing mark. That meant I had flunked out of school. If my final exam was 3 points higher I would have had a B and passed the course. I argued with the professor that the grade should have been higher but he would not budge. I officially was out of school. To get back in to the school the professor had to reinstate me. Then it is required to take the course again and pass it. He did reinstate me back into the school and I did sign up to take the course again. But by now I was ready to quit. I failed the course, failed the German exam and had to subject my family to poverty and roaches. My first impulse was to quit. But I have never been a quitter. I talked it over with Terri. She said that I could do it. She pretended the conditions did not bother her. So we decided to stay.

Then the professor who flunked me out of school must have felt sorry for me and did me a big unsolicited favor. Word had reached him that my wife would deliver soon and we were having a difficult time financially. He got me a part-time job with a friend of his analyzing boiler water. The job was for a one-man boiler water treatment company. It was owned by a very nice gentleman named Mr. Kyle. The job required me to analyze water. Also I had to visit customers all over the state, using the company car, to collect their water samples for analysis. It was an easy and relaxing job. It gave me the opportunity to see most of the state. The job did not pay much and did not completely end our difficulties. To get more money I began to tutor two high school girls. I received a grant from my Organic professor for the summer months. This was crucial for us to survive the summer. He was still trying to get me to convert to Organic Chemistry. But the greatest happening that summer was the birth of a new baby girl. Our daughter Rosemarie joined the family. She was special to us being our first girl. As she grew, Rosie was quickly becoming the apple of my eye. After having boys it was good to have a girl. Daughters are special to their daddy. All my kids were special to me but not quite like a daughter. School had been taking up so much of my time the past four years that I was breaking my vow to spend a lot of time with my kids. But I knew it was only temporary.

This birth brought a new difficulty to Terri. Many nights she either hardly slept or did not sleep at all. She was worried that the milk the baby drank might draw the roaches to Rosie's mouth. Then little Rosemarie might choke. As days passed, exhaustion overtook Terri and she began to sleep. Some of the family came down for Rosie's christening. Terri's cousin and my brother John were the Godparents. So Johnny and her cousin's families came down.

The second year rolled in much like the first except I saw Terri and the kids even less. In school we would have group meetings with my professor one night per week. I always was reluctant to speak even informally at this meeting. If I was the speaker I was my usual quiet, nervous self. I usually gave poor talks.

One night we invited my professor to dinner. He cornered my wife in the kitchen asking her to work on me. Her job was to get me to talk more. He told her I was smart and had things to say. Almost as an ultimatum he added that she had to work on me and get me to talk more or I would never succeed at a job. My ever loving wife did just that knowing how important success was to me. This fit in with her belief. The person that makes a good appearance and is a good talker does well.

I just could not find enough time to be with my family. My job and the tutoring ate up what little time I had left after studying. Also, another time consumer was me moving deeper into my research. I was deserting Terri with all the kids. She had all the work of the house plus raising the kids all alone. It did not seem to bother her. She was the kind of person that put others in need before herself. This was especially true if it was me, her baby. She said because I was trying to get ahead to better our family it did not bother her. If I was out drinking like my dad, then it would bother her.

During the course of the year my dad surprised us and brought the family down. He brought a lot of Italian goodies to eat. The entire family played board games together. We all had a good time. Dad and I went to play golf a couple of times. It was like a mini-vacation for me. Their stay was very enjoyable. For the first time since Frisco I felt like he was a father. The enjoyable time lasted two weeks before they went home. There was family togetherness like when we were in Frisco. Apparently his friends in Philly strongly influenced him.

After they left I went back to my research. I managed to do enough to publish a paper and co-author a chapter with Professor Reilley. All my courses were passed but I flunked the German exam for the second time early in the year and for the third time late in the school year. Again there were hardly any errors on my translations. The German Department allowed students to take a special test from a book of their choosing for a fee of ten dollars. I took this test from a volume of a technical journal. They selected the portion to translate but I selected the volume. This exam was passed. Strange, because I was sure that I had not done nearly as well as in my prior tests. Then I discovered the same scenario was happening to many students. They were only passing the paid tests. My paranoid mind led me to conclude that the German professors were using this ploy to raise money for their department.

There were other fun things to do at school besides playing football. We also had rats in the building. Some people would not think this was fun. At least it was a break from study and research. When someone spotted one of these nasty critters he would yell, "Rat". The office doors would open and the graduate students would come out running with hockey sticks or facsimiles. We would chase that poor rat up and down the halls beating him until he was dead. If nothing else it was a tension reliever.

On a day early in my third year I was sitting at my desk studying. Suddenly one of my books on the shelf fell completely apart. It was roaches at work. They had eaten the paste in the binder that holds the book together. The school roaches were a different variety than those at our home. These were black, much larger and stayed out of sight. They were even larger than those back in Philly. I was cleaning the mess when a fellow student came into my office. He asked me to go sign up for the French exam. I said, "Are you kidding I never had French." He replied, "What have you got to lose. You can take a dictionary and crib sheets. Besides, you can take the exam as many times as you wish.

So I went to sign up for it. It was scheduled a week later. I immediately went out and bought a dictionary, letter tabs and a grammar book. I put the tabs on every letter of the alphabet for a rapid means of looking up words. Next I made up a sheet of all the common words like "the", "a", all the prepositions, etc. Then I studied grammar for a few days to learn singulars and plurals, verb tenses and rudimentary grammar. I caught a break when the test came. It was on the invention of the oscilloscope. My familiarity with the scope and the inventor were a big help. I looked up every word and laid them out to make what I thought was good English sense. The result most surprisingly was that I passed the French exam on the first try. That was without ever having a course in the language. Yet I had three years of German with good marks and flunked their exam three times. Go figure it.

We went home for Christmas break. We were surprised to find my brother John was now an accomplished clarinetist. Unfortunately, he was acting weird. The way he talked and acted was much like a drug addict. The walls of his room were painted black and the ceiling light was covered with a devil mask. I told my parents he was probably on drugs. They got mad at me. As usual my mother was going through life with blinders on but my father was sharper than that. If they wanted to get mad at me, so be it. While home we went to Wildwood to see Johnny play for Wayne Newton who was just starting his career. Johnny was very good but nervous as hell. Later he told me that is why he started drugs.

My first job interview trip was scheduled while I was home for this Christmas vacation. It was a trip for me and Terri to the Olin Mathieson Chemical Co. in New Haven, Connecticut. The night before the interview, predictably, I was a nervous wreck. My hands were as cold as ice. Not only because I had to give a talk. But the head of the group and main interviewer was a man with whom I had been having a literature battle. The battle was over which of our similar methods was the better one. Terri did the best she could to calm me down a bit in our motel room. No matter what she did I was far from normal. She did get me to practice the talk with her. But she could not understand what the talk was about. My nervousness continued all through the night. I could hardly sleep at all. The next day I gave what seemed to me a not-so-good talk. In my estimation I gave a poor interview too. Shortly after I got home, their rejection was in the mail. It was either because of my interview/talk or our literature battle or both.

On my return I learned Mr. Kyle had a drinking problem. He would go on a binge most years at this time. His wife had a baby born dead at this time of the year. It depressed him so much that he became an alcoholic. Almost every year at this time he would go on a binge and wind up in an institution. I visited him as soon as I got word of this. He asked me to run his business for him while he was sick. I agreed and gladly did it for the nice man. This meant mixing his formulas on the floor with a shovel. Then the mixture is placed in a barrel and shipped. This while doing my regular job, the tutoring and school too. During one visit he told me how some of the townspeople had asked him how he could have a yankee, catholic working for him. His answer was that I was smart, reliable, dependable and the best worker by far that he ever had. That silenced those rednecks. Needless to say, I was super glad to know he felt that way about me.

The second semester was to be my last taking courses. It would not be long before we were not short of money for a change. It seemed we were always short of money despite all my jobs. To further aid our continual shortage I had a jar of pennies that I used to play poker with my neighboring medical students. I always won. This always supplemented our finances for the food bill. Many times we would not have eaten if it were not for those poker winnings. I also supplemented them by quitting smoking for a few months.

Every morning my car would not start. The starter was engaged with the flywheel and locked. I would have to go out and rock it until it unlocked. Sometimes I would have to push it too. With time this got harder and harder to do. We started looking for a car but just could not afford one. Finally I decided maybe I should sell it and buy a bike. I was only offered $25.00 by a car dealer and a new bike was $75.00.

Can you imagine my car and $50.00 for a bike. I had to do something to get a car. I did not want to take airplanes on all my interview trips if I could avoid it. So I devised a plan.

During the semester break I lined up several interviews. Two strings of trips were set up. One would be far from home and the other fairly close to home. The close one consisted of American Cyanamide, Union Carbide, Rohm and Haas, 2 DuPont sites, Esso and Mobil. These were all driving distance from my mom's house. So I bought a used car (a '57 Hillman Minx) and charged each company for the mileage from Carolina. With the money collected for the trips I paid the car. The companies came out even or ahead because they were not charged for hotels and eating.

There was never any intention on my part to work at Rohm and Haas due to the prior problems mentioned. I was also concerned that they would always look on me as Lou the technician. I took the trip anyway to visit my old friends at work. After I finished the first string of trips, my return to school was easier on me. All my courses were now finished. Further work on my research yielded a second publication. It now came time to take the Ph.D. exam. Fortunately I passed it on the first try. There was now little left for me to complete.

At work that spring I vastly improved Mr. Kyle's product for treatment of air condition tower water. As a bonus he purchased me new tires for my worn out set. My interview results trickled in and were now complete. They were all rejections except one. Even Rohm and Haas turned me down. I always wondered if my old boss, fearing I would come back to try to live up to my threat, had anything to do with the rejection.

Terri and I missed each other so much that when I came home from the interviews, she got pregnant again. The trip was not wasted however. It turned out that my only offer from the trip was $11,200/yr. It came from DuPont's Organic Chemicals Department at Deepwater, NJ. It was only about 50 miles from our parents. It seemed like a natural for me. It was close to home and was organic chemicals. So I accepted the job and cancelled my remaining trips. Years later my Division Head, Pat, told me that I did not do well in my interview and talk. Many people did not vote to hire me. He overruled them because of the way I put myself through school with a family. He strongly felt that showed physical and character strength plus responsibility. For these reasons he wanted me for his group. Also a student of Professor Reilley had an excellent chance of being good.

My Hillman began to have a similar starter lock problem with the flywheel as would happen to my former car. Every morning I would have to rock it until it unlocked. Sometimes I would have to push it like the other car. The problem with both cars was almost identical in nature. I began to wonder if it was me. One day, one of our female neighbors asked my wife if I bought a smaller car so it would be easier to push.

As the school year progressed I published two more papers in technical journals. This gave me a grand total of four papers and one chapter. Then a terrific thing happened. A new insecticide came on the market which killed our house roaches. The exterminators came to our house to spray. The results were amazing. The roaches actually dove from the walls dead. As we were getting ready to terminate our stay the roaches were all gone. It seemed just our luck to miss out on that joyous event. As the end of school was in sight I began to get itchy about money. The salary offered me was great. But all the years of hard work I put in made me want more. I began to look for different ways to make more money than my degree would offer. This desire was probably due to our years with no money. My first thought was to stay and go to medical school. The combination of a Ph. D in chemistry and a medical doctor would be valuable. Terri, who hated it there, said you can stay but without me. I would never leave my sweetheart. This ruled out my next idea which seemed a sure winner. The students at the school never had a good pizza and never even heard of a cheese steak or hoagie. A store that made these in good Philadelphia or New York style along with Philadelphia soft pretzels seemed to me a to be a sure winner. But again Terri said without me.

My two methods for making a load of money were shot down. Then out of nowhere Mr. Kyle offered me 49% of his business free, if I stayed and developed it. Terri was not so quick to shoot this down but she did. It did not really matter because shortly thereafter Mr. Kyle died. I would have never gone into business without him. His customers would have never dealt with a Yankee. These people were going to be the cash cow that would get us rolling. So if they would not deal with me there would be no business.

As graduation neared we were still having money problems. Terri did not want to see me work any harder. So she began a homecare job by taking in three infants. I urged her not to do it. She had three kids of her own and was eight months pregnant. That was more than enough. But Terri always thought she could do everything. But hard headed Terri had made her decision. She did it anyway. With three youngsters of her own and almost eight months pregnant she tried to help me by taking in three infants. She was that kind of person. All that work was too difficult for her. At the very end of her term she felt a strong pull about where the baby was located. She went in the hospital to deliver. I still remember them calling me in the middle of the night. They refused to tell me anything but just insisted I come to the hospital immediately. Their actions convinced me Terri was dead. I was scared to death.

When I got there the situation was bad but Terri was still alive. She was struggling because the baby was dead inside her. The news that Terri was alive relieved me so much that I am ashamed to say I did not care about the baby. But it was a baby girl who would have rounded out our family. She had strangled herself grabbing the umbilical cord. Now the problem was the dead baby was still inside Terri. The doctors had an extremely difficult time getting it out. Our neighborhood medical students were all there watching which normally would have embarrassed Terri. But she was in so much pain that she did not care. Eventually the doctors gave up and sent for a birthing machine at Duke University. They still had trouble but finally got the baby out. Poor Terri probably lost the baby because she tried to help me. Besides losing her baby, she had to endure all that physical and emotional pain. When it was all over I had time to grieve for our baby.

My thesis was completed in a split format between Gas Chromatography and analyzing mixtures by the difference in their reaction rates with a common reagent. The final step to get my degree would be the oral defense of my thesis before all the professors of the department. Terri and I took a positive approach to my passing this oral on the first try. Almost nobody ever flunked this oral. However we decided to take a financial gamble. The lease was about to come due on our house in Philly so we notified the real estate to terminate it. Then we drove back to Philly to leave our children at my in-laws house. This would allow us to take a leisurely trip back for my thesis defense. We could then arrange moving back without the kids in our hair. Our house would be vacated soon after we returned from my oral exam. Next we stopped at my parents' house to visit. There I got a big hello and "we knew you could do it". This from the two people who thought I was making a mistake. But now it was time for Terri and I to take a rest. After a couple of weeks we returned to Chapel Hill without the children.

I had not really rested at all. The oral was on my mind. The word oral meant I was nervous as usual. All the time I was driving back the test was on my mind. We finally made it back. The day of the exam arrived. I nervously got up before the professors. It was actually a relief to get the first question. My professor asked, "You're a gas molecule traveling down a molecular sieve column. What do you see?" Molecular sieve has a network of microscopic openings so it separates the molecules by size. Typically it is packed in a ¼-inch tube called a column. My professor expected me to answer about the network of openings. But I answered, "I can't see anything. It's too dark in here." Everyone laughed and for me the tension was broken. I went on to give a decent talk. When I finished I was told to wait in the hall while they discussed it.

I left the room thinking, they were going to discuss my defense and determine my fate. It was difficult to wait there while the minutes dragged by. The elapsed time hit

15 minutes, then 30 minutes, then 45 minutes. What could they be doing all this time. I kept thinking of answers I should have given. Flunking seemed a surety. The gamble on my house would ruin me. How could I tell Terri. I was a total wreck. All those years of school might be wasted. Then the door opened and one of the professors came into the hall. I asked him, "Professor Knight, how did I do?"

He answered, "You passed, Lou. I'm sorry, but we forgot you were out here. We were discussing school matters all that time." Suddenly it was like a pressure release valve went off in my body. I could not even get mad at them for forgetting me. I was now Dr. Papa. Quickly I took off for home to tell Terri the good news. Needless to say she was thrilled. We collected ourselves and notified the movers. Next we gave notice to the housing office.. Two days later the movers came. We had a very light load. We gave away a good deal of our old used belongings to the poor black people of the town. Then we went out for a celebratory dinner. In two days, the movers came to take our remaining belongings. Lastly we took our final drive home. Another big hurdle had been cleared by Terri and me. From poor beginnings I had elevated myself to a Ph. D.

CHAPTER 8

BEGINNING A NORMAL LIFE

The drive home somehow seemed more enjoyable this time. It was a good feeling to know I had accomplished the thing I set out to do. It would be more accurate to say Terri and I had accomplished it together. The Chemistry Department had given P.H.T.'S to the wives of the graduates. The letters stood for "Putting Hubby Through". Terri did not say much about it but I could tell from her actions that she treasured it. Although the Department intended it for wives who worked to support their husbands, Terri knew as well as I did that she worked harder than any of the other childless wives. I could have never done it without her support. Besides being my best friend, lover and confidant she was a very good cook, kept an immaculate house and raised our three children essentially all alone. She also suffered the misfortune of losing our baby at birth from trying to help me. As I thought about it, I had mixed feelings. Some guilt for what I indirectly caused her. But mostly admiration and thankfulness for all she had done for me. I just had to pull the car over to the side of the road to give her a big hug and kiss. I really appreciated all she did. Here we were married six years with four children born to us and more in love and devoted to each other than ever.

As I continued the drive my thoughts drifted to all the good things that probably awaited us in the years ahead. Now I would be earning very good wages. Our days of living in poverty were behind us. I would now at last be able to spend more time with my kids and loving wife. My school time had limited our time together from the very first week after our honeymoon. My mind continued drifting through all the wonderful things life would now have in store for us. I was going to do my best to advance at work to get things for my wife and children. The long ride home was tiresome as usual. My day dreaming finally came to an end. My mind came back to reality. Though it was tiresome, this time neither one of us seemed to mind the long drive. First of all there were no children clamoring or requiring attention. But the most important factor was this trip would be our final one. I had already decided not to go back for graduation. Doing so would make me miss time at my brand new job. I wanted to get off to a good start. This would mean my father would then have a perfect record for missing all five of my graduations. For the first time it would not be his fault. This time I was the blame. I seriously doubted that he would have gone anyway if I did attend it.

When we finally got home, our first stop was at my in-laws' house to see our children. I received a great welcome, almost like a hero. They presented me with a graduation gift and then we all celebrated. When all the semi-festivities settled down we went on to our second stop. This was my parents' house to let them know we were home for good. They gave me the same routine as when I came home before my oral exam. Funny, the people who thought I was crazy for going now said, "We knew you could do it". There was no big welcome like at my in-laws' house. To this day I never received a graduation gift from my parents for any of my graduations. But my parents finally admitted my brother Johnny was on drugs. He was now a professional musician and like so many others in that profession, he was on drugs. Maybe Terri and I had not done such a good thing after all.

After the greetings were ended, I tended to our primary concern. I called the real estate to find out about our house. They informed me that we could inspect our house for condition in one week. If everything was in good condition we could take possession a day later. At the inspection we found the house was very dirty and run down. The oven and range looked like they were never cleaned. We accepted it in that condition anyway. I refused to let Terri clean the range and bought a new one. We planned to do the home completely over again so there was no use haggling. Also we were anxious to be alone again. We moved in and completely renovated the house. I do not really know why but we bought Terri's parent's a new clothes drier and my mom a new clothes washer. Then I bought Terri a 1959 wide track Pontiac and parked it out front until she learned to drive. I bought life insurance and taught Terri all she needed to know about banking and otherwise running the house. It was my belief at that time that I would not live long. Leaving her with three kids, I wanted her to be self sufficient.

I came home on a Friday and taking no vacation, I reported to Dupont on Monday to work at Jackson Laboratory in Deepwater, NJ two days later. After meeting my supervisor, Division Head and the new fellow employees, my supervisor assigned me what proved to be a tough problem to solve. Then I received the painful, to me, news that an oral presentation of my work in graduate school was expected. This was an immediate blow to my nervous system. I just could not get away from those oral presentations.

The drive to work was tiresome. It was a poor way to start the work day. Then I found a carpool from Philly to work to relieve me of the constant driving. It required me to go a long way out of the way. I had to go almost completely around the city, making the drive a lot longer. But the carpool was worth it because there were five drivers and I only drove once per week. On my day to drive, I used the roomy Pontiac. The other four days I use my Volkeswagon to meet them, then I could sleep the rest of the way to work in their cars. At that point I appreciated the long drive. At work the day I dreaded finally came. I had to give my talk. In my opinion the talk was shaky at best. When it was finished I gave a sigh of relief. I had survived another one. The subject of my thesis was rather boring. I did not make it any better. As time passed I struggled daily with my tough problem at work. At home Terri and I repaired and repainted the mess our tenants left for us. We next carpeted the entire house and bought some furniture. Then, strange as it may seem, we began to look for a house in Delaware to eliminate my long drive. It cost us money but we were just tired of the living conditions of the past three years.

We were not home one year yet when my brother John called. It was the same old story. More trouble between mom and dad which frightened him. We went to their house to try to settle things. Terri was fed up and tore into dad. My mom was amazed she got away with it. At one point he tried to scare Terri by threatening, "I'll call your mother". Fearless Terri picked up the phone and said. "Wait I'll dial it for you". She dialed the phone and handed it to my dad. He hung up and they then talked calmly. My dad promised her that he would see a psychiatrist. My mom was again amazed at the progress Terri made with him and so quickly. My mom was never forceful enough with dad. Terri had always told her that and now had proof. After seeing the doctor a few times the Dr. concluded my dad was alright. It was my mom that was crazy for putting up with him.

We then received bad news that Terri's aunt had breast cancer. The poor woman had a double mastectomy. Her husband was a complete jerk about the whole thing and would not care for her. Her sisters were afraid to catch it and would not do it either. Terri and her mom volunteered. They took her into her mom's house to care for her. This meant daily trips for Terri. They changed the dressings daily and fed her until she healed. The woman died a short time later but at least she knew someone cared enough before she expired. Terri was always helpful to the needy.

Our house was now completely renovated but we began looking for one in Delaware. It may seem like a waste of money to fix up a home then look for another. But we were tired of the poor existence we lived in Chapel Hill. Also it would be much easier to sell the home and for a higher price. We quickly found a new home to our liking in a development in the northern Wilmington suburbs. We liked it enough to put a down payment on it. But we had to wait for it to be built. At the suggestion of a friend we visited this house often while it was under construction. This was to check on the workmanship and guard against termites by making sure they did not dump wood in the ditch around the basement walls. We also took his suggestion to hire a lawyer.

We visited the house almost every week for our inspection. At all of our visits we noticed that there were never any basement steps. This was curious to me. Finally just before settlement they were the last item installed in the house. Anxious to see why they took so long to install the steps I took a trip downstairs. The problem they were apparently hiding was a low ceiling. The distance to the floor was at least a foot too short. Also the floor had many wet spots all over it. There was a musty odor too. There were all the signs of a water problem which the builder tried to hide from us. They evidently could not dig deeper or they would hit water. Since they did not want to elevate the house, the result was a low basement ceiling. The property had a creek running close to it. This appeared to me to be the cause. Terri and I no longer wanted this house with its impending future water problems. It was a shame because we loved the house. But now we were glad we had a lawyer.

Because of this problem, we instructed our lawyer to terminate the agreement. We filled him in on the details of why we wanted to terminate. Nothing in our life so far was ever easy for us. But we still had each other. The lawyer notified the builder. At first, the builder resisted terminating the agreement of sale. But we had a house to live in so were in no hurry. We could wait longer than he could for the resolution we wanted. Finally our lawyer arranged a meeting at the property. Terri, I and our attorney met with the builder and his lawyer at the house. We all went down to the basement. Then just as though it were planned ahead of time or it was like a scene from a comedy movie. Our lawyer stood about six-six and their attorney about five-five. Then the comedy began as our lawyer stood between the basement beams which completely hid his face and then announced, "My client contends this ceiling is too low." Not to be outdone their diminutive attorney looked up at the ceiling and countered, "It looks heavenly to me." After a brief laugh, I commented that I was worried about a water problem. Then their lawyer surveyed the entire situation. He conferred with his client and convinced him there was no alternative but to return our deposit and terminate the agreement.

At the time that the agreement of sale was terminated I had worked at my job a few months and met many people in the area. This made me rethink where we should live. The people I met in Delaware were all chemists or chemical engineers. Many had masters but most had doctorate degrees. The area was loaded with people with Ph.D. degrees. To my way of thinking this would place an undo hardship on our children. Children usually try to outdo their fathers. It would be difficult enough with me having a Ph.D. But to be in a neighborhood completely surrounded by Ph.D. degreed people could be devastating to the poor kids. Besides, many of the people I met seemed too impressed with their degrees and stature in life. This was especially true of the wives. I felt absolutely sure that Terri would never fit in and be happy with the other wives. Many of the people seemed to worship DuPont. Wilmington smacked of a company town. Life there seemed to revolve around the company too much for me. We were not as cultured as most of the people I met thought they were. I saw trouble on the horizon and did not want my family subjected to that atmosphere. Terri agreed with me so we searched nearer to our home where the culture matched us better. I would gladly do the longer drive. It seemed to me Terri was owed that much. Unfortunately this meant giving up the lower property taxes of Delaware. So now I would have the high property taxes of New Jersey, my presumed new state of residence. But I would no longer be faced with the high state income tax of Delaware.

My first objective was to get on the Jersey side of the Tacony-Palmyra draw bridge. After a prolonged search all over south Jersey we found a home to our liking in Cherry Hill, NJ. Everything there suited our way of life better. It was still far from work but closer to our parents. The years away in graduate school made us want to be closer to them. By now I was getting accustomed to the long drive. My carpool had dwindled to me and one other person. We met in northeast Philly near my row house. After I moved to Jersey, he agreed to meet at my new home. This would eliminate, for me, the most time consuming and to me the most aggravating part of my trip. That was the Tacony-Palmyra drawbridge. This damned bridge seemed to be open when we got there most evenings and many mornings. We had to leave early in the morning in case it was open. Then it was open most evenings on the way home. This made our hours from 6:00 A.M. to 7:P.M. on most days. My carpool partner wanted to live in Philly for personal reasons. He agreed to meet me at my new home on the Jersey side. The drive from my new home seemed much easier to me. For a year it was on older not so good highways. But then a new super interstate highway was completed and opened. Then all of my driving was much easier. It certainly seemed a better alternative than living in a company town. At least it did to me. The drive would now be forty-five minutes. It seemed a small price to pay to give my kids and wife what I thought was a better place to live. A side benefit was that Terri would be closer to her parents.

Terri kept having high blood pressure problems during this time. I had to purchase the equipment to check it regularly. Then I took her to a recommended kidney specialist. He turned out to be a kid I played football with as a teenager. He wanted to perform exploratory surgery. We nixed that idea and dropped him. I just kept on monitoring her pressure regularly.

As time passed I finally got to spend some time with my wife and kids. It was delightful. For the first time I felt like a husband and father. But I was so accustomed to working long hours that I got itchy. Even with the good salary, money was tight for us. The expenses of the house, keeping two cars, the long drive to work, paying my college loan and raising the three kids seemed to take all our money. We rarely ate out or spent money on entertainment yet we always seemed to be short on money. This caused me to think of taking a second job. Terri would not hear of it. She finally had me home and said she wanted to keep me alive. One day while studying my check stub, I noticed how much taxes were taken out my pay. It became apparent that if I learned taxes more could be saved than by taking a nickel and dime side job. So I learned them and saved money.

At work, after a struggle, I finally solved my problem. Terri immediately asked if I would get a bonus. I remember answering, "They'll say you finally did what we've been paying you to do". During my first two years at work I made several unique solutions to problems. This impressed my Division Head. His name was Patterson but everyone called him Pat. One problem I worked on was a political one and required me to talk to upper management. It was apparent to me that Pat was now giving the most important problems to me. Pat was a great help in teaching me to speak better. Along the way I also solved two problems which resulted in publications. My supervisor transferred out of the group so Pat worked with me to improve my speaking skills. He was the one who hired me because of working my way through school with a family. I could tell he was glad he did. He started to treat me like a son. At my performance reviews he constantly prodded me to talk more and not be so quiet. He suggested I speak up more like one of our staff members did. I answered, "He is wrong often." Then he answered with words that stunned me, "So what, who knows the difference."

The thing Terri always told me was true then. Talk like you know what you're talking about and everyone would believe you. I found that concept hard to accept. In fact I never did accept it. I always measured what I am going to say and thought about it for accuracy before speaking. That is probably why I was always so quiet. Pat would always tell me, "You have important things to say. I always have to pry them out of you. Quit being so quiet and say them". Terri always sang the same tune. This tune was reminiscent of my graduate professor.

Then what turned out to be my big break came. Pat was put in charge of the analytical end of a task force to stop the government from banning tetraethyl lead (TEL), an anti-knock in gasoline. The idea was to produce data which showed exhaust from gasoline with TEL was no more harmful in producing smog than exhaust from unleaded gasoline. TEL was a very big money maker for the company. Therefore this work had the close attention of upper management. Pat selected me as one of the two analytical chemists to be in his group. Our job was to develop the methods that would be needed. We all transferred to the Petroleum Laboratory.

Our job there was primarily to develop a method which would determine the more than two hundred hydrocarbons in gasoline. There were also other methods needed. The primary method needed was to determine hydrocarbons in exhaust at very low concentrations. Our management knew that unleaded gas contained a higher concentration of aromatic hydrocarbons which are benzene and naphthalene derivatives. They assumed that these would appear at higher levels in unleaded exhaust. If so, they were known to cause worse smog and probably produce more carcinogens than leaded fuel. To prove this a make-shift method was quickly devised which we continually developed further to improve. This method would be needed to determine as many hydrocarbons as possible. The exhaust would be collected at the Petroleum Laboratory garage in very large polyethylene bags. This job would require many talks to the upper management and customers. This would give me good exposure for better or for worse. Although I quivered at the prospect of so many talks, I was flattered that Pat selected me and knew this exposure was good for my career.

In the early stages of this work it was necessary for me to go away for a week to visit government facilities in Bartlesville OK, and Cincinnati OH. It just happened coincidentally that the children were repeatedly sick. The doctor said their tonsils would have to be removed. I thought we would have it done when I returned from my week long trip. But to spare me the time and worry Terri had it done while I was away. She took the kids for the operation all by herself. She felt I had enough to concern me. She was that kind of thoughtful person.

During this period we were having trouble at school with my son Michael. His 3RD grade teacher contacted Terri for a meeting. When they met she revealed that he was very disruptive to the class. Continuing reports revealed no improvement. We were at our wit's end on how to handle him. We were not accustomed to any of our children being a behavior problem and would not tolerate it. Many threats of punishments did not succeed. This did not sit well with Terri and me. We were disciplinarians from the old school. Finally her temper roared and she threatened no Christmas for him if he did not improve. I was sure this threat would bring improvement so I did not object. But when he did not improve we felt forced to uphold the threat or lose control. So we held his presents back until he improved his behavior. This created quite a furor with the grandparents. I thought it was somewhat harsh but he had his chance to avert it. I only mention this because my son recently told me that we lost him that day. It obviously bothered him a great deal, but not enough to be good in school. Perhaps we did lose him that day because he was habitually a problem for the remainder of his early years. I had trouble with him in the boy scouts. Later he took up drinking beer and drugs and wound up in a rehab center. We had no idea it would have this impact on him and it is still difficult for me to accept. But if I had known, we would have never done it. Who would think a person would ruin a part of his own life over that punishment. But then, he was only a third grader at the time, not an adult. Today he is free of his demons and seems to blame it all on his mom when I should share an equal portion of the blame. I can not accept that this caused him to ruin his early life. At any rate he is living a normal life now and is a great help to me. As a parent now, I hope he understands that once the threat was made we felt we had to go through with it.

On the lighter side one thing I always liked about this period was my daughter Rosie greeting me on the front steps as I came home from work. She would give me a complete report of the day's happenings. But on the darker side of things, Terri and I got concerned about my brother Johnny's drug problem. He claimed he was ready to break the habit. Terri felt my parents were not doing anything to help him. She felt sorry for him. She was always ready to help someone. It was now his turn. She suggested that we could help him break the addiction if he came to live with us. This would get him away from his friends and fellow addicts. For a short time, we thought everything was going well. Then we discovered every drug in our medicine cabinet was gone. He had stripped us clean. To add to this the local pharmacist told me he was stealing non-prescription cough medicine from the shelves. Johnny and I had a talk. He told me I should never believe anything he tells me where drugs are concerned. As an addict, he would do anything for drugs. We could not have our kids grow up around him. So we shipped him back to my parents. We failed to save him.

About this time my oldest boy was about to join the cub scouts. I volunteered to be a leader both to keep my promise to myself to work with my kids. A side benefit to me would be speaking before audiences. The exposure was limited but helped a little to conquer my fear of appearing before audiences. A year later my second boy joined. I thought the two years of facing audiences helped conquer my fears a little. But my first talk for the company was at a seminar in Detroit before members of the government, oil and automotive industries. Also this would be my first experience using a microphone before a large audience.

I was at my all-time worst as far as nerves were concerned. As my turn to speak came due, my hands and fingers were cold as ice and numb. The people conducting the seminar called a break at that moment. This break in the action temporarily saved me. I gave a giant sigh of relief. But I quickly realized it would soon end and I would be in the spotlight again. So as a waiter came by with a tray of Martinis, I grabbed one. Me, who until that time only had one alcoholic drink my entire life. The Martini numbed and calmed me down enough to get me through the talk in reasonably good fashion. In the ensuing months I gave many talks at work. Pat always drilled me before hand. The talks were for our management and for some of our customers. So, of course, he wanted me and himself as group leader to look good. As the talks mounted I got better and more at ease.

It was now, more than ever, evident to me that giving good talks was necessary to get ahead at work. I decided that I could maybe accomplish this by pretending I was an actor. When I thought about it, I decided that giving a good talk is just like acting. My boss gave me the tools I would need. He taught me how to organize the talks for maximum effectiveness. From then on I got better at it. Pat was an excellent speaker. He was a great help in teaching me all the mechanics of giving a good talk. He showed me how to arrange the talk, make the slides and how to use a pointer without it shaking all over the screen. One of the best things he drilled into my head is do not be afraid. No one in the audience knows as much about your subject as you do. In all his teachings, some of Pat rubbed off on me. The exposure in scouts helped conquer my fear of audiences. Learning how to organize the talks followed by actually giving many talks made me a better speaker. Sort of as a climax, before one of my talks, I passed one of the big bosses in the hall. He asked me how the "golden throated orator" was today. At first I thought he was kidding but then I realized that the bosses would not have sent me to speak unless they thought I did well.

At home things were going well now. I was active in the Cub Scouts and we had a lot of family togetherness. Then Terri got pregnant again. She told me at the moment of conception it had happened. After so many pregnancies I believed she would know and was probably right. She was right as evidenced by her missed period and morning sickness. So we began to have sex au natural. Then about three weeks later she told me she got pregnant again. I do not know why I did not believe her this time. I did not think it was possible so I told her she was crazy. Then it never entered our minds again. Her pregnancy was quite a bit different this time. She was much larger and had a sort of shelf where her stomach was located. She could put her plate of food on it when she ate. She was definitely struggling more too. We still never gave that earlier event a thought. Then lo and behold seven months later to our complete surprise her bag broke. I took her to the hospital where she had twins that night. They were a boy and a girl. Terri felt God gave her back the girl she lost. We named the boy Tom after my father-in-law. Then I insisted we name the girl Teresa after my wife. She had her Lou should anything happen to me. Now, if anything ever happened to my wife I would always have a Terri. I am sure my father felt badly that we skipped his name again. He deserved it.

At work that week our secretary filled in the weekly accomplishments for me. It read; only accomplishment this week-twins. I was highly concerned about how Terri would react to all the work involved in caring for twins. For this reason I took no chances and sold my gun. Not long after the birth of the twins Terri became an insulin dependent diabetic. She had long been a borderline diabetic. Her family had a history of it. Probably the stress of all the pregnancies, the last one being twins, tipped her over the edge. But unexplainably, her blood pressure now became normal on a regular basis. But we both decided we better do something to avoid further pregnancies. She wanted to get her tubes tied. The doctor told her she should wait six months because it was a major surgery. So she planned to have it done in July. I did not want her to go through surgery. She had done enough carrying six babies. Just then I heard of a new operation (at least it was new to me) to sterilize men. It was called a vasectomy. I investigated it through my medical doctor cousin. It was a rather simple procedure. She had done enough in my opinion. I had to protect my Terri. She had all the children. Now it was my turn to do something. Without telling her I went to see a doctor and arranged for a vasectomy. My idea was to protect her from getting pregnant again and to avoid an operation which may be dangerous for her

A little over a year later, at work, I completed the final development of my method for exhaust. It was a gas chromatographic method which determined more than 260 hydrocarbons at the one part per billion (ppb) level. For the uninitiated 1 ppb is equivalent to finding 1 second in the time since Christ was born or 1 pea in a line of peas from New York to London. This was quite an accomplishment in the 1960's. It would not be such a great fete today with the new chromatographs, columns and detectors. The giant study performed by DuPont using my method on exhaust from leaded and unleaded fueled cars was now complete. My method and its predecessors were used for all the analyses. Results, as our management suspected, showed unleaded exhaust was slightly worse for smog and carcinogen production. But TEL was later banned anyway. Actually for a more serious reason which should have been obvious from the outset. It caused the emission of lead into the environment. That was reason enough for the government to ban it.

As far as speaking went, I felt sure I had come a long way. Then, after a talk I gave on my method before the Society of Automotive Engineers using of a pointer and a microphone. I found out this was correct. At the finish I felt the presentation went well. Then a relatively young engineer from Ford approached me. He said, "Gee you gave a great talk. I wish I could be as calm as you." I thought me calm! I could not believe it. My acting worked. His comments meant a great deal to me. To me it signaled I had finally made it from the kid who buried his head in his mother's lap. This method led to two more publications. The paper was up for a $1000.00 award but I came in second to an engineer. I never expected to win. An engineer was bound to win at their symposium.

However at my performance reviews Pat continued to tell me that I do not talk enough at meetings. This was my next area to conquer.

On the home front, a few years were spent as manager of my sons' Little League teams. I enjoyed it even more than the year spent managing Terri's and my brothers' team. One day stands out in my mind. At work that day six hundred thousand pounds of smokeless gun powder blew up at a neighboring plant. The entire building that housed my laboratory shook. I put on my helmet on and went under my desk. After a couple of minutes it seemed safe to come out. I realized the company would shut down phone lines. I figured they would shut the Philadelphia line last. So I quickly called my mother. I told her to call Terri, explained what happened and I was fine. It was a good thing I got through. The blast was felt all the way up in Cherry Hill. Neighbors heard what had happened and came to comfort Terri. But she assured them I was fine. We had a little league game that night. When I got home my two boys were in their uniforms. Michael said, "Don't worry Dad, if you were killed, we weren't going to play tonight." That was cute.

It was special coaching baseball with my sons this time. When that finished, my oldest boy now joined the Boy Scouts. As usual the scouts were short of leaders. We started a new troop at our new school and I signed up as the Scoutmaster. The following year my second son joined. We had many trips both camping and to special places like Washington D.C., Gettysburg and Bull Run. I had a lot of fun with them and would not trade the experience for anything. This was just another way I fulfilled the promise made to myself in my early years. The experience of playing with them, camping with them and just attending the weekly meetings while watching them grow was priceless.

One thing I always took heat for from my kids was the way I reprimanded Tommy one day when he was somewhere between one and two. My wife put him in his crib upstairs for a nap. He kept climbing out and running downstairs. Finally she got tired of dealing with him and turned him over to me. He kept doing the same thing to me. Each time he was put back and spanked. There was also a danger of him running down the stairs. As he continued I could not have him defy me and be exposed to danger. I certainly did not want to keep spanking him. That was accomplishing nothing. No matter what I tried he would not listen and stay in the crib. This defiance had to end. He had to learn that I was the boss. Finally, at my wits end, I got some clothes line rope. I made a harness used for rescuing people with knots I learned in the boy scouts. I was careful to make it loose fitting. Then I attached it to the crib slats so he could not sit or stand up. I went outside the room. I left the door open a crack so I could watch him to make sure he would not get hurt. He struggled for a while but finally gave up. I went in to see him. He said he would stay in bed so I removed the rope. In a short time he fell asleep. My older kids thought this was mean. They still mention it today. I still can see nothing wrong with it.

My daughter Rosie was a very good softball player. I never seemed to have time to be a leader at her events as I did for the boys'. There were several reasons. First I was so involved with the scouts and Little League that I simply did not have any more time. Also I felt uncomfortable coaching girls. Then her team had a coach who never would have surrendered the job anyway. Still I always felt bad about it. The same was true later when my daughter Terri played. I had continued involvement in Scouts and I was then coaching my son Tommy in Little League. Attendance at every game that was possible for me was all I could manage for little Terri. I hope the girls did not resent me for the difference in allotted time. Rosie later was a star player in basketball and soft ball at her high school. Her mother and I were very proud of her when she won a college scholarship to Temple University for soft ball.

A couple of events occurred while my boys were teenagers that help show more of the characteristics of Terri. A neighborhood bully told my son Michael that the only person he was afraid of in Cherry Hill was Mike's mom. The second event occurred when my two sons witnessed a gang of boys trashing another boy's car. My sons were witnesses for the police. The gang threatened them not to testify. When a school hall monitor tried to intercede they trashed her car and threw a cement block through her living room window. These boys were tough and ruthless. My boys were obviously scared. Who could blame them, we were all scared and worried. I tried to get the word spread that I was a chemist. If anything happened to my boys I would place the same horribly stinking, almost irremovable chemical used by gangsters in the 1930's for the protection racket. It was valeric acid. Those boys treasured their cars so I hoped the threat would be effective. I do not know if that word ever got to the gang members or if it did, did it have any effect. Terri on the other hand arranged a meeting of the boys in the gang, their parents, the vice principal of the school and the police. When all were gathered she stood up and declared words which I will paraphrase since I do not remember the exact words. "If anything happens to my boys, something will happen to these boys too. You will not have to look for who was responsible. It will be me." I do not know if either threat had any effect, but nothing further ever happened. This was an actually physically weak Terri at her norm. She was fearless and very protective of her loved ones.

Now I was highly successful at work. Besides that I kept the promise of time for my kids that I made to myself when I was young. Tommy had no interest in scouts. We did go camping together one time. The cold weather began to bother me like never before and it was not really that cold. I chalked it off as getting older. Camping became too much for me so I quit the boy scouts. The promise I made to myself was kept by spending time with my sons as their Little League team manager, their Scoutmaster and one of their Cub Scout leaders. For my daughters I was only a regular attendee at their games. I often wondered if my sons appreciated what it took for me to do all this or did they think I was just a meddling father out to spoil their fun. Perhaps I made a mistake. Maybe they should have been exposed to someone else. But if I did not share these experiences then I would have missed out. I also wondered if my daughters thought too much time was given to the boys.

Work slowed down now that the exhaust methods were in place. It was a routine analysis now. Then the moment I had hoped for came. I was offered a promotion to my choice of two supervisory jobs. One was to be in charge of the Analytical Research Group at Jackson Laboratory where I started or at the Petroleum Analytical Laboratory where I worked to develop the exhaust method. Most of the analyses in the Petroleum Laboratory were routine established methods. So the job was really to supervise that routine operation. The choice then to me was no contest. The one job was research which I found much more challenging and exciting. As a member I simply loved that group. Taking that job would give me a chance to improve the group which in my opinion it sorely needed. So I chose the research group, hoping to make this group superior to most.

Shortly after my promotion was announced, my father-in-law died. I was always glad he lived to see my advancement. He and I were always good friends and he admired me going to school. He was all for education having gone to night school for years. It was rare to find a man that came to this country at nine years old who now had no trace of an accent. This man showed appreciation for my accomplishments and let me know about it. He was more of a father to me than my dad. As mentioned, I was glad he lived long enough to see me promoted. Also he knew his daughter now had a nice home and was loved by her husband. Terri, as usual was a helping hand, took her mother in to live with us. It did not last too long. They could not live together so her mom went to live with her son's family.

My youngest brother, Albert, was now finished high school. He had no direction in life and no self esteem. He was not independent and there were rumblings that Johnny was trying to get him on drugs. Terri again came to the rescue. She suggested we take him to live with us and steer him. He had saved some money from his job. It was the same job I formerly had, working at my aunt and uncle's drug store. We first urged him to get his own checking account. He was either afraid or too lazy to open his own but we made him do it. Next we suggested he get a cheap used car. Then we pushed him to get enrolled in college. His high school marks were not good enough to be accepted by a college. So, I suggested he go to night school where he could get accepted. Then if he got good marks, they would accept him as a full-time student. I suggested he take Algebra, which he was poor in, while he was living with me so I could tutor him. He had enough money left to pay the first semester's tuition. When classes began he got home late from school. I picked him up at the train depot then took him home and tutored him in Algebra. This did not leave me much time to sleep but it was worth it. I could see he was doing well. When he successfully finished his first year, he was accepted into day school. Now he had built some self-esteem and independence for himself. It was now safe for him to go back home.

At work I had been doing well as a supervisor. The hardest part of the job for me at first was facing the chemists for their performance reviews. But I learned to prepare well for them and give them fairly. The most difficult reviews for me were for the chemists who were doing unsatisfactory and needed to improve. The hardest of all was terminating the employment of three chemists for performance below DuPont's standards. Two were there when I arrived and were already performing below the company's standards. The other joined the company shortly after my arrival. Despite the terminations we all parted good friends. As part of my job, I managed to do research with a couple of the chemists in my group leading to joint publications. I even was invited to write three chapters. One was in a Chemical Dictionary. Then my Division Head was transferred and replaced by Pat. He was my boss again. Luckily we got a new manager who was willing to request money to equip a top notch group. So as things evolved I had my chance to get things more to my liking.

As I looked over the division the main thing wrong in my opinion was we needed a strong chromatography leader. We had three groups. One of the supervisors retired after a heart attack. I got his group to go along with mine. This just made it harder for me. Then I convinced Pat to reorganize the division to get all the gas chromatography under my supervision which was easy. Pat was already convinced of my chromatographic prowess. I now had the research group, chromatography and all the spectroscopic methods under my direction. To do this I got the gas chromatography section of the Division's third group. I now had most of the division under my command. Next I reminded management that we had good chemists and paid good salaries. Despite this we got poor results because of our poor equipment. That certainly is a waste of money. We needed to spend our money more wisely. It would be better spent for good equipment. We already had the correct manpower. Now we had to equip them properly. We purchased a couple of new gas chromatographs, a gas chromatographic computer system to give accurate quantitative results, a state of the art gas chromatograph/mass spectrometer (GC/MS) all to replace our old obsolete models. Our old systems were absolutely poor. Those simple moves, which initially cost a good deal of money but ultimately saved money, made us the best chromatographic group in DuPont. Overall the two best analytical groups were probably my group in Organic Chemicals Department and the Plastics Department group. I now had a giant group.

At home things were making Terri and I very happy. Raising the twins was very exciting all along. My brother Albert graduated college. My father honored him by attending his graduation. It was the first graduation that he attended of any of his children. He must have had some good luck gambling too. Not only did he attend the ceremony but he gave a small luncheon for our family members.

The early years with the twins were especially enjoyable for me. I had missed those early years with my other three children because of school for which I will forever be sorry. Terri enjoyed it too because there was something special about twins. Now in a blink our first three were on the brink of becoming teenagers. We had two families now and with that came two families worth of noise. The younger twins had their own band of friends with their own brand of noise. Then the older three were becoming teenagers with their loud music. The combined noise often got to me. I jokingly told Terri that a block away coming round the bend from work the house could be seen shaking. It was apparent that the noise and the long drive to and from work were starting to wear me down as my age advanced. The large group I always talked myself into supervising did not help. But to the kids I was now branded a grouch.

At work things were going rather well. When there were explosions in the plant, my group had to do round the clock wipe tests to analyze for toxic contaminants. We had rotating shifts. Not wanting to ask my chemists to do anything I would not do, I took my turn at doing these tests even in the middle of the night. I had good rapport with all of the members of my group both technical and non-technical. We even had a technician-chemist basketball game in which my sons were the referees. The increased number of technical papers and chapters put my total technical articles published at 14 and my total chapters at 5. This now got me listed in "Who's Who in American Men of Science". Mention of that brings up an interesting event. Terri came to the prestigious Gordon Conference in New Hampshire with me. The wives would get together for daily activities. On this particular day several of them were boasting about their husbands as scientists. One of them got the bright idea to see how many were listed in the Who's Who. So off to the library they went. Terri was surprised and proud to learn I was the only one listed. It silenced those bragging women. Until then I did not even know I was listed.

From 1968 to 1978 were the happiest years of my life. I refer to them as my teenage years. That is mainly because I never had teenage years. Terri taught me to dance. I even learned to jitterbug although I was never any good at any dance. That was the Disco era and I was best at that. Terri and I went dancing often. She loved to dance so I decided to take Cha-Cha lessons from a neightbor. But either because I was too bad and a stiff dancer or I may have aggravated an old football knee injury, I wound up on crutches.. But perhaps it was the beginning of future health problems. At any rate Terri and I enjoyed that period of our lives. If I had to guess it was her favorite years too. But toward the end her complications of the diabetes started to arise. Poor Terri now had diabetic retinopathy and had several laser surgeries to slow down the progress of the condition. Nevertheless the doctor told her it would lead to blindness. He gave her five years.

Getting back to work, I later discovered that Pat now told our Research Director that I was an internationally renowned Chromatographer. A transfer was now offered to me within the plant. The plant had a complete water purification system supported by an analytical laboratory. My name came up as a possible person to do this job. The manager of the entire operation interviewed me to be head of this laboratory. Strangely enough I was formerly this manager's supervisor. He decided that he wanted me. I really did not want to leave my group so I volunteered to do both jobs until we could identify someone to do the job. There I was biting off too much again. Now I had over one hundred people reporting to me.

Shortly before this, our Research Director swapped jobs with the Research Director of the Plastics Department. Then the manager of the Plastics Department Analytical and Physical Measurements group announced his retirement. His replacement was identified as one of their Senior Supervisors. The new Plastics Research Director asked the new manager who he wanted as a replacement to do his former Senior Supervisory duties. The new Manager replied they really needed someone strong in Chromatography. The Director said he knew just the guy. Remembering that Pat had labeled me as a world renowned chromatographer, he identified me as a possible candidate for the job. The new manager then arranged to come to my laboratory to meet me on a ruse. He came to ask about our newly purchased GC/MS. It was an instrument which cost more than $100,000. His group was in the market for one so they wanted to know all about ours. They asked many questions trying to learn about the instrument and our experience with it. As it turned out it was all a pretext to secretly interview me and see how much I knew.

Happy with what he found out, he passed the information to his Director. They had now identified their choice for a new Senior Supervisor. Their Director contacted the new Organic Chemicals Director who had just come from the Plastics Department. The new Organic Chemicals director promised to grant his wish. So I was offered a promotion, raise and transfer to the Plastics Department at the Experimental Station in Wilmington. I unofficially rejected the offer through Pat and onto our new Director. Pat would be retiring soon and wanted me to be selected to replace him. Pat told me as much. That was the job I really wanted. My love for Jackson Lab. and our division was strong. I wanted to benefit from all my accomplishments and do more. The new director could not understand my attitude. He made it clear to me that I had to accept. When I asked Pat what would happen if I did not accept. He guessed I would be transferred to some remote place like Beaumont, Texas. That threat scared me enough. So I accepted the job. With it I got a raise and a promotion.

At my going away luncheon I ribbed all my chemists about leaving them in a money making plant while I go to what we jokingly called the country club - the Experimental Station. But I was not happy about going. The job I loved would be left behind. The high Delaware state income tax and the bridge tolls everyday would eat into my increased salary. The result was I actually made less take home pay. So I was unhappy but I had a nice office and a good group, Terri thought I was nuts. Maybe she was right, I was toying with high salaries and had upper management staring me in the face. I was on the threshold of big bucks.

CHAPTER 9

THE WALLS BEGIN TO CRUMBLE

While she was pregnant with the twins Terri's doctor put her on thyroid medication. The apparent result after the birth was a large weight loss. After the birth of the twins, Terri was the same weight as when we got married. Then after she became an insulin dependent diabetic the doctor took her off the thyroid medication. He said she had to stop because of her insulin. Slowly she gained all her weight back. Clearly there was something wrong with her thyroid. Her maternal grandmother had a thyroid problem too. That poor woman had a goiter and died at age 53. Poor Terri could not win. Many of her past generation relatives had diabetes and her grandmother had a thyroid condition. Genetics were against her.

Meantime I had a new job at the plush campus called the Experimental Station in Wilmington Delaware. No longer would I have to deal with the problems of an old dyes and intermediates plant. There would be no more explosions and no more calling on my analytical group to do wipe tests for toxic contaminants. My job would be much easier on me now. But still I was not happy with the move. Love for Jackson Laboratory, the friendship I had with all the people and that type of work were now a part of me. The action of the plant was exciting to me. My old group members were all close friends. I had built the best or second best analytical group in DuPont and wanted to continue making it better. But I was moving to the group that rivaled my former group. The biggest negative was my take home pay would be reduced.

I was lucky in an important respect though. The people at my new job were all very nice too. I had no complaints on that count. The new group was the other best or second best analytical group in DuPont. The new job was really a good one. All the people were likeable. The secretaries were nice girls who were good at their jobs. I had a decent office too. The atmosphere was more like a college campus than an industrial chemical company. New hires had a great preference for the Station rather than a plant. If they were offered jobs at both sites they almost always chose the Station. Most DuPont employees preferred the Station too. I seemed to be the only odd-ball that preferred the plant. I longed for my old group and the action that occurs at a plant. Terri thought I was crazy. Maybe she was right. I should have been but I was not happy. When Terri heard what the Station was like she wanted her baby properly outfitted. So she took me out to buy several new suits.

Not long after I had settled in to my new job, my brother-in-law had a serious nervous break down. He underwent a complete change in personality. He ran away from his home then from me and many other family members. We were all unsuccessful in stopping him even to just talk. The change he underwent greatly affected me. My arm began to have a numbness or dull ache near the shoulder. It reminded me of some symptoms for a heart attack that I had learned. But later I would find out it was a brewing disease. So to be sure I went to the hospital emergency room to have it checked. There were no signs of any heart ailment so I was released. His break down and personality change had a bad effect on my system. I could feel it. After all he was more like a brother to me than my own brothers. He went in a local institution for a short time, then came to live with us for a short time.

Shortly, things settled down enough for me to do a decent job at work. Joe was put in a mental hospital in Philadelphia. Terri and I made many trips to that aggravating place to visit him. We wanted to see how he was doing and check on his progress. It is a certainty that this was even harder on Terri than on me. She evidently was emotionally stronger than me and took it better. Finally they let him out pending visits to a psychiatrist. Terri and I felt sure what set him off in the first place was his wife. She was a real bitch. She was abusive to her children and had many weird sexual ideas. We could see that she was getting to Joe. But he would not open up to anyone and let his feelings be known. He just rocked in his chair and stewed. Finally they sent him back to live with her. In our opinion he did not improve in the next few weeks at home. In fact, we thought he got worse. So one night I called his doctor to ask if it would not be wise to hospitalize him again. The doctor replied that was not possible because Joe was not a danger to himself or anyone else. The next night Joe stabbed his wife and inflicted a wound on himself too. That shows how much his doctor really knew about him.

After that grave incident he came to our house with his son. When he told us what he had done, I thought he must have been speaking incoherently. I just could not believe what he said had happened. I immediately called his home to check on his wife. His wife or her family had already called the police. The police were already at his home. When they found out he was at my home, two detectives hurried to our house. Joe was arrested in the foyer of my home. His nine year old son who had come with him asked why they were doing this. When we explained to him that his father had stabbed his mother. The kid began to clap and cheer. That gave us a picture of what the mother was like in the child's eyes. We had seen her abuse to all her children before but especially to him.

Joe's first stop was the Camden city jail. This was no place for Terri to visit so I visited him almost every night after dinner. Unfortunately, a friend of ours that was a lawyer insisted on taking the case to work on getting Joe help. Letting him handle the case turned out to be a big mistake. He was incompetent in my opinion. Most of the time, I had to tell him how to handle the case. Eventually, Joe wound up in the Trenton State Psychiatric Hospital which is really a jail for the criminally insane. It was a real hell hole. In my opinion no one could get better there. At first we could only visit in booths where you talk to each other on telephones. This was an ungodly place that I think only made people worse. Terri and his mother visited him often. Because of work I only could go on Saturdays. That was enough to upset me. I could only imagine what it did to the women and especially to Joe. His mother's efforts got us to visit where he stayed. The guys on his floor were real whack-os. The thing he had done was awful but he did not belong with these guys.

During his stay the other inmates stole his clothes often. Terri was buying him new outfits just about weekly. To make matters even worse the doctors could not get him to take his medicine which impeded his progress. I tried hard to convince him to take the medicine. There was no getting him to agree. Finally I put his son in his place as a model. Then I pointed out how much he would want the boy to take it. I paralleled this to the same way his mom wanted him to take it. After hammering this home to him, he finally agreed to do it. Once on the medication he rapidly began to show improvement.

During this period Terri kept having problems seeing. She was diagnosed with diabetic retinopathy. Her only hope for saving her sight was to have laser treatments for her eyes. And the doctor pointed out that there was a very slim hope of permanent success. A temporary fix seemed to be the best to expect. The situation looked liked eventual blindness was a certainty. As could be expected, Terri was terrified. At that time her mom was also having medical problems and trouble living alone. So we took her in to try living with her again. I presume her difficult to live with actions were partly because she was ultra-concerned about her son's plight and partly because it was her nature. Her son was a prince to her. On the other hand Terri always took a distant back seat. Terri was my problem. Her mom kept aggravating Terri. Poor Terri was having enough problems and concerns about her health. She was getting her laser treatments routinely. But still, there was the specter of probable blindness facing her. This I know scared her to death. But it did not stop her mom from aggravating her. The woman was also bothering our twins. Finally I had enough. One night when she was lying in bed I went up to talk to her. I discussed her treatment of the twins and aggravation of Terri during her trying eye problems. I asked her don't you care about your daughter's eyesight. When she answered me no, calm Lou disappeared. I yanked her out of bed and ordered her out of our house. The twins and Terri were happy I finally did it.

All the time Joe was imprisoned his mom worked feverishly to get him out of there. The lawyer was useless. We eventually fired him. After about a year his mom achieved her goal. He was moved to a private hospital. After a stay there he was released as long as he visited a psychiatrist. Joe now came home. His mom and he got an apartment together. He continued to do well as long as he was medicated.

In other goings on in the family my dad seemed to be getting somewhat concerned about leaving something to my mom when he died. In retrospect he may have even been thinking he would die soon. He was a real flim-flam man that collected everything. He told me, "I feel sorry for you when I die. You're going to have to get rid of all my stuff. Instead of insurance I have a lot of valuables in our safe deposit boxes. You're going to have to sell them for mom." He told me the location of the boxes. Then he took me to a gemologist/jeweler friend of his where I could go for appraisals. Either as payment for what I had to do or perhaps to ease past guilt he then gave me a piece of jewelry as a present. It was a piece I had admired. It was a gold nugget on a gold chain, for neckwear. A small diamond was set in it. It was a nice piece that I liked. He then gave me tips for places to get rid of the gold, silver and gold coins in his collection. I never gave any of these instructions a thought at the time.

My body began calming down so I could do my work. I had been doing traveling to the Department's plants. It was their policy to have me go to the plants to meet the personnel in charge. Then when a problem would come up that my group could possibly solve they would be familiar with me and my group's capabilities. Unfortunately for me, the plants were in out of the way cities. They were in places like Parkersburg, WV, Belle, WV, Camden, SC, and one good city. That was Houston, TX. My trip to Houston, TX and a conference in Atlanta were the only places I could take Terri with me to relax her from our hectic life. While we were in Houston, I purchased a ten gallon hat and cowboy boots. Cowboy movies and equipment were a childhood love of mine. They were a hit with the people at work when I wore them there on my return home. The people in my new group and the secretaries learned just what a goof-ball I could be.

Our Department now merged with the Elastomers Department to form the Polymer Products Department. A little later we merged with the Film Department. This added Circleville, OH to my plant visit schedule. The consolidation of the first two Departments eventually put me in charge of 49 people both technical and non-technical. There I was biting off too much again. Most of my time was now spent preparing performance reviews for all my people. To me, this was the most important thing in my job. To be with the new people my boss now moved his office to the Elastomers building. I am sure he was confident I could handle everything in my building. It consisted of all people in my group. This got me a move into his vacated more luxurious office.

My raises were excellent and I continued to get a bonus every year. The bosses at Jackson Laboratory were probably correct when they told me, as I left, that a good career awaited me. I now had a plush office with a scenic view of the Brandywine creek. My window view was of the water rushing past and forestry across the creek. The office and view were so nice that I took Terri and the kids to the station to show them where I work, what I do and meet the people in my group. My family was duly impressed with the office, the computers and instruments of my profession. My second son was so impressed with the computers that he later became a successful computer programmer. Aside from my travel to remote places, I was beginning to like my new position. The places were so remote that commuter flights with small planes that scared me had to be taken. Using my tax knowledge I took a few steps to make my pay actually increase instead of decrease. Now I was happier. Things were moving smoothly.

I did get a chance to show every one at the new job that I was a "hands on" person. Our Circleville plant was in dire need of an analytical method, quickly, for a trace toxic contaminant. The Hewlitt-Packard Company sold a bench top GC/MS that I was sure could do it. It cost about 50,000 dollars. I quickly located a "demo" that I could get quickly for a reduced price. I arranged to buy it, rented a truck and drove to Circleville with my mass spectrometer man as an escort. We arrived and set it up in one day to make sure it was in working condition. Then we flew back to Philly. The next day I sent my gas chromatography man to develop the method. He worked on it for several days with no luck, even with repeated calls to me. I told him to come home and I went there. In one day I developed and set up the method for plant use. That showed the station people how a plant trained man can work.

The group I now supervised was probably one of the two best problem solving group in DuPont. My former group was the other. My new group was strong in spectroscopy whereas due to my input my former group was strongest in Chromatography. I was picked for this job to strengthen this group in Chromatography. If I were successful, my new group would be the best problem solving group in the company. As a supervisor dealing with people I seemed to be doing rather well too. Word got back to me that many people in my former group and in the present one too had told others I was the best supervisor they ever had. My salary was growing. The brass ring was within reach. I was on the threshold of the big time.

Just when things were settling down from Joe's crisis another tragedy struck. This time my father was murdered.

After the funeral, at my mom's request, she was going to move into our house. We now took in another boarder. Terri could just never say no to a family member in need. Word of dad's murder was all over the news. It was on the radio, on TV, and in the newspapers. The story was repeated over and over again. The media dug out his whole sordid past and reported it in detail with their own spin on it, to make it a god story. Among other things he was reported to be a fence. That was one of the kindest things said about him. I was angry at first. But on reflection I could not blame tne reporters. I was angry that it had to come out. How could I blame them, it was all true. It was my dad's fault. It was their job to do it. Now I began to think about my dad's recent actions. He must have known danger awaited him. We emptied the safe deposit boxes and found much jewelry, coins, gold, etc. Since he only had two thousand dollars in insurance, this was all my mom had in the world.

I selected an undertaker that just took over for his dad. Their parlor was right near my uncle's drugstore. I knew his dad and him since he was a little kid. When Terri and I went to make funeral arrangements with him I noticed he kept eyeing my nugget. Also he was wearing a good deal of jewelry. This looked like a good opportunity for a trade. I explained that my mom had no money. Further that my dad had little insurance but left a good deal of jewelry. He would have to wait until I sell it or, if interested, we could make a trade.

The nugget would be included in possible selections for the trade. I decided to give up my nugget for my mom. He was interested. We then arranged a night when he could have a jeweler friend come for appraisal purposes. I brought several pieces on the designated night. The final selection was the nugget and one small, not too expensive, diamond ring for his wife in exchange for the complete cost of the viewing and funeral.

Back at work, I felt the publicity surely brought any hope of my career advancement at DuPont to a crashing halt. I felt sure that this news, coupled with the fact that I lived far away and was not one of the in-crowd would end my chance of further advancement. Besides those obstacles, I was now outspoken and may have rankled a couple of bosses for things on which I was right. I certainly was no politician. Further I did not think the higher echelon in Wilmington would tolerate a person with my now publicly known unsavory family background to advance to upper management. That sort of mentality is one of the reasons I did not want to live in Wilmington in the first place. I now felt I would no longer be on the threshold. The brass ring had eluded me. Funny, my mother-in-law did not want me to court Terri for things she heard about my father back when I was a teenager. Surely time showed that she was as wrong as my management might be.

Despite my dislike for my dad's behavior, the murder hit me harder than I would have expected. Visions of identifying the beat up face linger till this day. The combination of Joe's crisis and dad's murder seemed to throw my whole body out of kilter. I was not sure what was happening to me but something changed the way I walked and my ability to think as clearly as previously. At home, our three bedroom house was now overcrowded. My mom needed some privacy. So Terri went shopping for a house. She found a four bedroom house to our liking. In fact it was the model house we originally wanted to buy in 1964 but we could not afford it. We purchased this to accommodate my mom. The deal I made with her was she should add the money from the sale of her home. This along with some investment profits I had made would allow me to buy the new home cash. Then she could live there free the rest of her life and I would pay the sizable tax and utilities increase every year. I insisted on paying the house cash because it was evident to me that my health was failing in some way. I did not want to leave Terri and mom with a mortgage.

There was some happiness in the next two years to offset some of the previous pain. My brother Albert got married to a nice girl named Marianne that year. To show his appreciation for what I had done for him, he asked me to be an usher in his wedding. I was at least seventeen years older than the other people in the wedding party. Next my older two sons got married the year after dad died creating more room in the house. My daughter was in college. The house was now emptier than ever. Terri and I were losing our children. The weddings were happy times but were followed by the reality that our kids were leaving the nest. This brings a somber reality highlighted by the fact that we are getting older. The house got quieter like we always yelled for but it signaled the end of an era. We were getting older like it or not. Before we even got accustomed to losing two boys to marriage and a girl to college Michael's wife presented us with our first grandchild, a boy. He was a little Mike. Talk about feeling old. Terri was now a grandmother at only 42. A little later Marianne's parents invited Terri and I to dinner. That was a surprise and must have been somehow due to Albert or Marianne. They were nice people and lived on my medicine delivery route when I was a teenager. A little later still Albert decided to go to graduate school at the University of Virginia. Marianne's parents, Terri and I, Albert and Marianne rented a truck and moved all their belongings to Charlottesville VA, the site of the school.

Just about that time DuPont decided to get out of their outside analytical business which I ran as part of my job. It involved the entire division not just my group. One of the small companies which we supported begged the people in my group who did the analysis to open their own business to continue the analysis for them. The analysis would bring in lucrative fees. The two people came to enlist me as a partner. From there, they wanted to expand the business. We all reasoned that there were many small companies left out in the cold by DuPont's decision. My knowledge of all the customers plus their familiarity with me, because of running DuPont's business, would be very helpful in this venture. We hired my oldest son to do the analysis. He was going to school to be a chemist so we could trust him to do the analyses.

Their idea hit me at just the right time. Not only did I hate paying the large Delaware income tax. But now I felt my career advancement had ended. It sounded very good to me. However, I would not try this without first getting permission from the company in writing. This would give us some form of protection. So I got a letter from the company allowing us to open such a business. We purchased an instrument for $20,000. to do the analysis to start our business. In a short time we completely paid the loan. We then began to save for more equipment.

My suspicion about my career now seemed to get confirmed. Although I can not honestly say it was because of my father. It may have been due to me. Possible reasons could be my nonpolitical outspokenness, my living distance from the in-crowd, a combination of these or some other reason. My boss was promoted to another position. I was passed over as his replacement. The job happened to go to a close personal friend of his. He seemed very uncomfortable when he informed me. He gave me the lame excuse that although I knew the analytical half of the division I was not familiar with the physical measurements half of the division. Yet they replaced him with a man who did not know either half. He was not an Analytical Chemist. But in fairness he was a highly competent manager type chemist. But this was a blow to me. It came after 21 straight years of glowing performance reviews for me. In every review I was rated outstanding. My boss had entrusted me with a good portion of the division too. I thought it had to be my father's ghost although it could have been any of the reasons mentioned above. When my boss told me, I did not handle it well. Usually I am quick to grasp what is being said and come up with good answers. But it seemed to escape me that I was much more qualified. I just ranted that I really did not want his job. I wanted to get rich with my new business. Sour grapes, if I ever heard them. I let him off the hook too easy. While he was giving me the bad news tears formed at the corners of my eyes. That was very unlike me. Something was happening to me. I had no idea what it could be.

The new boss was not with us long. But when he gave me a raise, which is automatically tied to the rating on our performance evaluation, his comments convinced me that I earned more than he did. That is not surprising since I was older, had more service and was always rated outstanding. But I got the feeling it bothered him. Later that year he dropped my rating from outstanding to very good. It was the first time in my career to fall from the top rating. However I did feel It was deserved. Whatever was bothering me health wise was slowing me down physically and affecting my ability to think. At meetings I felt bewildered an unable to effectively grasp what was being covered. I had difficulty concentrating. I could not blame it on my boss.

A couple of months later my boss was transferred and a new, even younger, man was promoted in his place. Again I was overlooked. This time I did not care at all. At least he was an analytical man. Also, I was beginning to feel too sick to perform. The job would be too much for me now. The new business was occupying more of my time now too. Terri and I had recently purchased a house in NJ to rent to my son Michael and use as a tax shelter for us. Before he could move into it he changed jobs and no longer wanted it. My company now decided to use that house as our laboratory. We paid me. It was also a nice place for Terri and I to visit on some weekends. I could work and we could use it as a get-away cottage. The business was doing well now and we had six pieces of equipment. Unfortunately I was not doing well. I had balance problems. While mowing the lawn I fell overturning the mower. Luckily I did not sever my feet. I was always banging into walls and falling over things. At work my secretary thought I was drunk. The business and my career had little significance to me at this point. I was more concerned about my health.

Then on a trip for DuPont to attend a conference in Williamsburg Virginia, I took Terri along. We stopped at

Washington DC on the way back and visited Georgetown. While walking over cracked pavements I had enormous problems lifting my feet high enough to get over the small ridges. I even bumped into a lady in a drug store. When explaining it to my wife, I blamed the lady. But Terri told me it was my fault. In our hotel room I flopped on the bed scared stiff and cried. Here I was crying again. I never cried before. What was wrong with me. Did I have a brain tumor? Terri was highly concerned as was I. Terri was highly upset. Something was seriously wrong with her baby. She tried to comfort me. Meantime she continued to urge me to see a Doctor. Until now stubborn me had resisted going. Now it was very clear to me that I should go for my sake and Terri's. So I promised to go as soon as we got back home. She drove the rest of the way home so I would not kill us or someone else.

We then began a long tour of quite a few doctors. Terri and I made visits to at least eight doctors. The first doctor was an ear, nose and throat man. He sent me for a CAT scan. Then would you believe they could not read it. So I had to go to a highly respected neurosurgeon to read if I had a tumor. There was no tumor. That was a relief. Our ex-family doctor was next. He thought I was a psycho case. A number of doctors followed. I underwent a barrage of tests aimed mainly at the ear. The tests uncovered nothing. The doctors seemed mystified. No one could diagnose my condition. Finally I took my blood sugar at home with my wife's test kit. It was a shockingly low twenty. Then we went to my wife's endocrinologist who we knew to be a real smart doctor. He confirmed my low blood sugar. He labeled me as hypoglycemic. A special diet followed much like a diabetic's diet. The diet worked. But the doctor warned me that it may return. He added the words, "We have to see if the hypoglycemia is fanning something or something is fanning it. Looking back, I think he suspected my problem but wanted to be sure.

In my mind my problem was diagnosed and cured. Therefore I returned to work with my usual vigor. One of my partners decided to leave our company. So my other partner and I bought him out for his portion of our current worth which at that time was $12,000. We now took my remaining partner's son, who was a CPA, and my oldest son, who was finishing college to be a chemist, in as partners. My goals now were to get my rating back to outstanding and to beef up my business. A distant hope or dream I had was to retire from DuPont and run my own business. This seemed real to me with my son becoming a chemist.

But after a few more weeks past, all of the symptoms of my condition returned. Thoughts of leaving DuPont and it's benefits were dropped until I could find out what was wrong with me. Then, they might have to be dropped forever. Now I went back to my wife's doctor. He acted like it was probably what he suspected. But he did not say anything to me about what it might be. Instead he sent me to a neurologist. So he did suspect what was wrong with me. The problem was not his specialty so I guess he wanted to be sure. The new doctor seemed to know quickly but ran a few physical tests to be sure. Then the neurologist diagnosed me as losing the myelin coating from my nerves. The next day at the library at work I discovered that was Multiple Sclerosis. Evidently the doctor wanted to deliver the bad news in small doses. Next visit he gave me the bad news. Now I thought the highest hurdle in my race of life had been reached. There are only a few things that can be worse. Reading the symptoms of MS cleared up the things that were happening to me. They were: loss of balance, emotional instability leading to easy crying, problems with weather, to name a few. These explained my falling and tripping, my crying so easily, the numbness in my arm when Joe first got sick and the problem I had with weather when I went camping with Tommy.

The disease seemed to get worse rather rapidly maybe because I now knew what it was and what it would do me. There was also my worry for Terri's and the twins' future. My world seemed to be collapsing. Then I also got bad news from my boss. Another chemist in our division got enamored with the success of our business. So he now asked permission of DuPont to start his own business. He heard we were now moving into a field he pioneered and wanted to get in before we could establish it. DuPont's reaction was to withdraw our permission to operate the business. They offered to buy our equipment so we were not stuck with it. I felt we could still operate the business outside the sphere in which DuPont had operated so I only sold them the piece of equipment for the field the other chemist had pioneered. I, will forever be sorry that I did not take that offer. It would have been about $50,000. Because of my debilitating illness I no longer wanted to leave the safety of DuPont's benefits. But I still thought I could keep alive the idea of my own business. I believed I could do it with my pension to back me. My partner and I now wanted to keep that one lucrative analysis as a cash cow and later branch out into fields foreign to DuPont. After all, owning my own business was a life-long dream of mine.

My plan faltered almost immediately. The lucrative analysis we did was for a business that was on a government contract. That contract now came to an end. The number of samples submitted slowed drastically. The business began to sink. Matters continued to get worse. I had a minor auto accident. Then one evening when I got home from work, I exited the car with my brief case in hand. The weight of the brief case pulled me down the drive way into the street. I went into the house. I sprawled on the floor and cried. Poor Terri became highly upset.

It became evident that it was no longer safe for me to drive. Fortunately, one of my car pool members who lived close to me volunteered to drive my car on my day. In addition my disease kept progressing rapidly. My group at work was located on two floors in our original building and due to the merger in another building a long way across the station and up a big hill. It became just about impossible for me to visit my people. My judgment and thinking ability were diminishing too. I asked my young boss to replace me because I could no longer do my job effectively. He was sympathetic and wanted to create a new job for me reading over methods in the entire department and reporting on them orally. But I was already walking with a cane, could no longer write, could not focus my eyes fast enough to read at close to a normal pace and was beginning to talk with a bad slur. They would be wasting their money was my answer. A trip to the company doctor verified my poor condition. He recommended I retire immediately on their disability plan before I get hurt. I am sure he had in mind that I would then ruin their safety record. When I left Medical I met a girl in my group. I was very unsteady probably from the retirement news. It pained me to need her help but she helped me back to our building. She spread the news to some of my group. I was sitting in my office, my head being cradled by a secretary. I was crying and saying farewells when my wife called to inform me Louis' wife presented us with our first granddaughter. Terri thought I was crying over her news but I told her I had to retire. Baby Jaclyn was born on that day. I also retired that day.

CHAPTER 10

RETIREMENT ON DISABILITY

My highest hurdle so far had been reached. I thought none could be higher. And so my retirement on DuPont's disability program began. The company had two plans. If you were disabled you would get 25% of your salary. If you were totally and permanently disabled, which I was not yet but would be soon, you would get 60% of your salary. That was a large difference which would greatly affect us. DuPont sent a departmental personnel man along with my boss to explain our benefits. The man had never been through this before and was absolutely no help to us. He was completely unprepared. We were in a fog as to where we stood. Terri got so frantic that she called the president of DuPont. She got his secretary, so explained our situation to her. The secretary told her not to worry. She was absolutely sure that as a member of management I would get the larger benefit. The personnel man came back at a later date to explain the benefit to us.

During the visit, he mentioned that my wife cost him his present job. He had been transferred because of the way he handled the situation on his first visit. I am not sure if it was due to my wife's call or my boss' unhappiness with his first visit. I heard from friends that my boss was very unhappy that the man was completely unprepared. He could see how worried he left us. My boss passed this on strongly to their boss. But since the man said that my wife cost him his job, I suspected it was due to her call.

At any rate, I found out the benefit would reduce my salary to 60% of the original salary in 1983. The 60 % was made up of my pension, social security disability, and the remainder made up by DuPont. The three portions were roughly 1/3 each. Terri and I were very thankful for that benefit. We would have been lost without it. We would have been forced to sell our home and move to a much cheaper residence. This would have meant uprooting our twins and completely changing our lifestyle. That is the main reason I did not leave DuPont to work full time on my own company. Thank god I never made that move. All my grandiose dreams were probably dead now. Our finances would be tight to even approximately maintain our standard of living. These benefits were essentially stagnant. Only the 1/3 Social Security portion would have small annual cost of living increases. The company benefit along with owning the house clear made our existence possible. But it would still be tight because the property taxes were very high and escalating every year. These taxes plus the utilities were equivalent to a high mortgage.

All that was going through my mind now was our complete financial position. It would be difficult if not impossible to maintain our standard of living. We would not be able to put the twins through college. Everything looked very bleak to me. It bothered me a lot that I had come so close to making good on all my promises to Terri to travel when we were older. She struggled so hard when we were young. Throughout my whole life I wanted to do good for her. Now I felt like an utter failure. These facts and losing my career hit me hard. A deep depression hit me big time for about a year. The doctor prescribed mood elevators and anti-depressants.

Of course I was not a failure. I had come a long way from my beginnings. I had many good accomplishments. But ever since I fell in love with Terri, doing things that would please her was always my main objective in life. The methods I desired to do it were no longer possible. At first, all I did all day was lie on the couch in my depression and watch TV. A soap opera was on my viewing menu. This is something I never watched before. They always made me want to upchuck. I was feeling sorry for myself. To add to it the drugs the doctor prescribed were making me like a Zombie.

Finally Terri said enough of this. In her take charge manner, she flushed the drugs down the toilet. Then she said, "You have to get up and we have to face this. It's here to stay." I knew she was right. We made plans to get me moving. First we had the doctor order a physical therapist three days per week. It was a good female therapist. Then, I began her therapy. Also using a cane as an aid, I began to continually walk through the house in a big circle. Fortunately we had a large house that was laid out perfectly for the circular walk. My record was 33 times around the house.

It thrilled me when I reached 33 times. It seemed ironic that once I was a good baseball and football player and now I got excited to walk around the house with a cane. But when the exercises began the number was growing. I was gaining which thrilled me. Then I began losing ground with time. Then it started to get harder and harder for me to do. But I wanted to keep moving so I would not suffer atrophy. My depression returned because of realizing I would only get worse with time. I used to go to meetings and lunches at MSA. Watching the people who had MS longer than I did struggle and drool depressed me too much. I pictured myself getting that way in time. That depressed me further. The therapist next switched me to a walker with wheels in front for safety reasons. I just hated all forms of exercise because it hurt and was a terrible strain. When trying to exercise my weakened right side I strain so much, I felt like I was going to have a stroke. My kids all think I am too lazy. My track record shows I was never lazy. Then we lost the therapist because the Medicare coverage ended. So I switched to walking with the walker with Terri nearby me in case I needed help. My wonderful wife was always there to help me. I began to fall often. I feared almost everything especially getting a shower. When I fell Terri got frantic with fear. We had to call our kids to get me up if they were available. If not, it was the rescue squad. This was not the golden years I promised Terri.

I now purchased a computer to keep my brain functioning. My manual dexterity was limited so I could only play simple games like card games, chess and checkers. I also used the word processor to try my hand at writing novels. As time progressed I reached the point where a wheelchair was necessary most of the time for me to move around. My deterioration continued but not nearly as fast as in the beginning when I was working. MSA gave me a manual wheelchair. Now my ever loving Terri went out and bought a mini-van. She insisted we have some form of transportation so that I do not sit in the house all the time. So we equipped it with a wheel-on or drive-on lift. The problem now was I had to rely on someone to push me. Terri had a bad back so I would not allow her to even attempt it. My arms were no longer strong enough to wheel myself. When we went out friends pushed me. This insulted my independence. Plus often men left me facing walls while they talked to someone. Life in a wheelchair was not fun. First of all you develop a sore rump from sitting so long. Then a feminine hazard always awaited me in the casinos. The casinos were our only form of entertainment. In the crowded casinos women going in the opposite direction would pass on my left side with their handbag swinging on their left arm. The bag, unknown to the woman, would often club me on the shoulder or head. It depended on her height. The women probably never realized this was happening. There is so much happening in a casino that their attention was undoubtedly diverted.

Some of my former workers started to visit me all the way from Wilmington. It thrilled me that they thought enough of me to make that long trip. They came to my home 2-3 times a year and took me and Terri out to lunch at first. Then Terri volunteered to make lunch to save me the traveling. These people even came to visit me during my hospital stays. One of the older and better chemists told my wife that I was the best boss he ever had. He and his wife were fans of Dr. Carlton Fredericks. Based on his philosophies they recommended Bioflavonoid tablets for Terri's eye problem. She began taking the pills. Over time they seemed to stop the progression of the condition. Her doctor had predicted five years to blindness only two years before she began to take them. Whether it was due to the pills or an unlikely remission her condition seemed to stop progressing. Her eye doctor was amazed. He made a note of it for possible future treatment of patients.

The company my partner and I founded no longer had that lucrative paying analysis to do. This gave me more reason to be depressed. My original partner and I elected to close the company. My dream was approaching death. The company had $20,000. in cash in the bank. Like a dope, I could not let my dream die. We decided on a split $18.000. for him. I would get $2,000. and all the equipment. I still had hopes. The equipment was still at my rental house where my daughter and her girl friend were living. I still had hopes of doing something with it. My older son was still my partner.

I made another try with therapists. This time it was at the Kennedy Hospital. A lady friend of ours took me there twice a week. They were well equipped so we accomplished more than when it was at my home. But, as before, it became more and more difficult to do the exercises. When Medicare's coverage ended I was glad. About then Terri and I received very disturbing news from two friends. My mom had told each of their mothers that she really did not want to live with us anymore. After all we did for her, we were hurt. We gave up our house and greatly increased our expenses. She denied it but we knew it was true. The mothers of our friends had no reason to lie. I caught my mom in many lies about that time. We treated her very nicely. Many times we took her to Atlantic City to see shows and her favorite singer. Terri was always pushing her to go out and do things with her. Terri took my mom every where with her. Terri's friends became her friends. Maybe that is what she did not like. After all she was a sort of a recluse.

Then one night she got excited over a fight Terri had with little Terri. We were having friends over for dinner that evening. During the dinner with our friends, my mom walked out. She told my daughter to tell us she left to go to my sister's house. There were no good-byes, not a word was said to us. We were highly upset. When my sister called to tell us she was there, Terri was upset. She answered tell her not to come back. It may have started as a misunderstanding but we never heard from her again. I was once her golden boy. We loved each a great deal through all the years. But now she was deserting me. We never heard from any of my family again except my sister's kids. This did not sit well with me. Terri got very bitter over this incident. She could not believe that my own family, who I helped support through my teen years, could now ignore me when I needed support.

My condition had now deteriorated to the point where I could no longer go upstairs. I had to sleep on the sofa. We had get a portable commode for me. Terri was now stuck with cleaning that. It bothered me more than the disease itself that I was doing this to her. I wanted to die. We needed to build a downstairs bedroom and to enlarge our downstairs powder room to make it a full bath. The bath had to be equipped with bars for the handicapped. After purchasing the van we did not have enough money left to do all the necessary renovations. My daughters were good enough to offer us a loan to make these improvements and install ramps. Then my oldest son loaned us money to buy a Craftmatic adjustable bed. I was now all set to live the life of a truly disabled person. This just killed both Terri and me. I was always such an active person, now I could hardly move. Terri took it very badly to see me so disabled.

The construction took long to complete because the builder worked too infrequently. When it was finally finished I purchased a power wheelchair. This chair's list price was $5400. At the time it cost the same as a Hyandai. Fortunately my daughter Rosie worked for an insurance company and had connections with the right people. She was able to get it for $3900. Medicare paid $2700. so we only had to pay the balance. Soon thereafter the disease which had diminished our sex life, completely ended it. I was only 53 and Terri 50. To not be able to please Terri was the worst part so far for me. I tried almost everything available on the market to restore my capability. There was very limited success. Finally I gave up hope. I realized that even if my capability was restored, I could not move much. Terri was very unhappy with our plight but she never complained. I heard of many cases where wives in similar situations left their husbands. I offered her the chance to do the same or to get herself another man. She almost hit me. She knew I was always very jealous and would suffer if she did. Besides, she was insulted I would even think of that. Kissing and just touching each others skin, which we loved to do anyway, became our substitute. I guess that is what true love can do. Not all was black back then. There were happy events in this period too. Michael's wife had another baby boy, our third grandchild Matthew. This was later followed by Louis' wife giving birth first to Samantha and the next year to Louis Jr. We were now blessed with 5 grandchildren.

One thing that always bothered Terri was to see someone, usually a man, in a wheelchair that looked unattended. This really bothered her. She would always say, "The poor man looks like no one cares about him. He's still a person. He should be cared for by someone." She always took excellent care of me. She dressed me well. She cleaned both me and my chair often. This was necessary because my uncoordinated hands would drop food all over me and the chair.

My son and I discussed the future of the business. He could not handle the analysis load alone with a family and a job. So we decided to add a new man with a full partnership. The young man was his friend from college. His name was Mike. Both of the boys had just graduated college as chemists. Louis' job was with an environmental company. He had knowledge and contacts in the growing field of water pollution. Analysis would be needed in this field. Our plan was to move into the field of water analysis. Mike was trained to do microbiology work. He would be our man for all such work. He had not found a job yet so he had lots of time. We decided to name our company Aquanalysis

Before we could get started Louis landed us another lucrative paying analysis through a friend of his. It was the analysis of sulfite on grapes. This is the residue left from fumigating grapes with Sulfur Dioxide to kill mites. We purchased the equipment necessary to do the analysis which was minimal. We even rented a place to be our laboratory. Just then, Mike found a job. With both boys now working days and me being immobile there was no one to pick up the grapes. When we got rolling a dependable person would be needed for any analyses and grape sample pickups. Mikes had a dependable brother. He was currently unemployed. We made him our fourth partner. He planned to stay with our company if we were successful. Later we could teach him all the analyses but his immediate job would be to collect the grape samples every day. Since money was now coming in at a good rate, I loaned the company $10,000. to purchase a piece of equipment that would be vital to water pollution analysis. An Atomic Absorption unit for trace metal analysis. This was our last bit of money and turned out to be another mistake on my part. But Terri wanted to see me occupied and happy. She would probably soon replace it. She was super at saving due to her bargain hunting. She came up with money most of the time. She had paid the loans to our kids and amassed the money rapidly.

Our partner, Mike, related an interesting event to me that occurred when he was job interviewing. He was having difficulty finding a job. Then when interviewing at Mobil Oil he mentioned that he was in partners with Lou Papa. The man in charge said if you are good enough for Lou Papa you are good enough for us. So he hired him on the spot. The man was one of DuPont's customers who visited me to learn of my method for exhaust and also heard my talk to the engineers in Detroit. Mike was sure happy that the man's knowledge of me and my work got him a job.

It seemed I was just destined not to have a successful company. For some unknown reason we lost the grapes analysis. Then as time went on, I just could not function very well at all. We had designated me as the man to get us new business via telephone. But by now I could not hear well or speak very understandably. The people I spoke to seemed to get frustrated trying to speak to me. They probably thought they were talking to a moron. Most potential jobs eluded me. Our income went to zero. Finally Mike and his brother elected to dissolve the partnership. Mike because he just got married and needed the time. His brother just needed a paying job. At this time Louis and I gave up running the business too. My dream ended. At this late date we sold all our equipment. Some we had purchased new and some were used. They were now all varying ages but used pieces of equipment. We got the paltry sum of $12,000. The market for used equipment does not pay much. Originally everything cost $60,000. for the new and used. To think I could have sold it to DuPont for $50,000. but did not do it. That turned out to be a very bad decision on my part. Now since I loaned Aquanalysis $10,000. to buy the piece of equipment for metals analysis, I was only getting $2,000. out of the sale. So the original three partners got 12,18 and 2 thousand dollars. I was the big loser.

The next years dragged on but seemingly sped by. My life consisted of sitting in front of the computer and either trying to write books or playing games. Most week ends two friends of ours took us out to dinner. Everyone had to help fat me into the van. Terri had to struggle to help me in the van. She also struggled to get me in the shower three times per week. I fell sometimes. As I said before showers, which I loved so much, were now a fearful adventure for me. When I fell, we would have to call one of my sons or my son-in-law or both. You see, I gained a lot of weight from sitting immobile in the wheel chair. Although I ate less than before it was evidently still too much for my present situation. This made me difficult to handle for the strong young men. I was impossible for Terri to handle. These events unglued Terri. She did not know what we were going to do. She wanted to help me but could not manage me.

It had reached the point where I was now afraid to get a shower or go out in the rain because I would slip trying to get on the van. Unless someone strong was there I became afraid to get in the van when the ground was wet. The once fearless football player now became a fearful person. I was now afraid of almost everything. It bothered me most when I fell because it upset Terri so much. Plus I fell so often that I was bound to break something. We now called two boys because they both developed bad backs. It would not be such a strain if two were there. Throughout this illness Terri went out of her way to make me comfortable. She saw to it that early on I went to therapy then exercised regularly when that ended. She saw to it that I was always clean, that I went out regularly, she bought me loads of clothes and shoes. Would you believe for a man who can not walk I had five pairs of new shoes. Despite my unmanageable weight she would buy me treats. She loved and simultaneously felt sorry for me.

CHAPTER 11
THE CRUMBLING FINISHES

There were some good times in the 1990's too. My son Michael took a second wife named Debbie. Then they had a really cute little daughter named Angela. She was born premature and was very tiny. When my son's family visited us from the south, she was such a tiny cute kid. I can still see that cute little girl running around the house with her short legs. Now she is a tall long-legged teenager. Later in the decade my oldest son Louis got remarried to a sweet girl named Tiffany. Then my daughter Terri fell in love and married a great fellow named Bill. Her twin brother Tom married a sweet girl named Diane shortly thereafter. Terri and I were happy with all their chosen spouses. Soon we loved them all too. I did manage to get to all the weddings despite being in a wheel chair and not feeling very well. Soon more grandchildren came on the scene. One was immediate. Bill had an 11 year old daughter named Kat from a former marriage. After they were married a year or two Tiffany gave birth to a beautiful baby girl named Madison. She soon became the little darling we played with daily. I had many songs recorded on my computer. She would dance to them for Terri and me. We were now rich with seven beautiful grandchildren.

To offset this happy scenario of the '90's I was having some medical problems. The problem was somehow related to my urinary track. It plagued me through most of the decade. The problem was always the same. In many evening I would get a fever which would have a drastic effect on my MS. It would make me completely immobile. This made things extremely difficult for Terri. The urologist always diagnosed it as a urinary track infection caused by the improper emptying of my bladder which he said was common with MS patients. He would prescribe the powerful antibiotic 500 mg. Cipro. Lesser strengths and other common urinary antibiotics did not work. The Cipro would immediately knock it out whereas the other medicines we tried earlier were ineffective. The infection and fever struck me every so often at first. Then after a while I was getting it about every two months. Then it got to be monthly. The frequency increased a little at a time until it reached weekly. I was having a difficult time functioning during this period. Tommy got married at this time. I had to go to his wedding feeling awful but I made it.

About this time my mother died. Although it was tragic to me to lose her, I had not seen her for more than twelve years.

I had not heard from my brothers and sister either. I could not bring myself to go to the viewing or funeral.

By now the frequency of my urinary events was bothering me quite a bit. No one else I knew with MS had this problem. I became skeptical that doctors use the easy out of "due to MS". I switched doctors with no real luck in getting to the bottom of my problem. Simultaneous to this, I would periodically get blood on the toilet paper when I wiped my rear. Since the blood was bright red I dismissed it as hemorrhoids. I also had the embarrassing misfortune of dropping a load in my pants one night. This happened when I bent over to release my wheel chair footrests to get on the toilet. My wife was away that day so I was forced to call little Terri and Bill. To me this was the height of embarrassment. My wife then forced me to go to a gastroenterologist to check out my condition by making me an appointment. He ordered a colonoscopy. At that time Katie Couric of NBC was doing a special on TV on colonoscopies. I did not expect any connection between my two problems but I remember telling Terri "nothing good will come of this". The doctor performed a colonoscopy which revealed a malignant tumor in my colon. When he told me, the words were paralyzing. He said it would have to be surgically removed. Then he recommended a surgeon. A visit to the surgeon and a CAT scan were next.

It was now March of 2000. So I began the new millennium with an operation for cancer. Terri was petrified. There was a problem cleaning me out the night prior to the operation. I could not do it at home so Tommy called an ambulance and off to the hospital I went. The hospital personnel had to give me an enema. My son, Tommy, stayed with the young man to administer it. The water went in but did not come out. So, the boy gave me another one. The result was the same. My abdomen was now swollen and hard. Evidently we waited too long. The tumor seemed to be too large now. My son pressed on my abdomen but only a little of the fluid came out. My other son, Mike, joined Tom in the middle of the night. The two of my sons stayed with me all night and tried to press the fluid out to sweep me clean. The tumor apparently blocked the water from exiting. The operation was a success as far as removing the tumor was concerned. But because I was not cleaned out properly the surgeon had to leave me with an ostomy. He told me the tumor was the size of a softball.

This now seemed to be a possible answer to the frequent urinary track infections. The large tumor may have been pressing on the bladder preventing it from emptying properly. It also could explain the bowel movement in my pants. Next the surgeon had sent my lymph glands for biopsy and we awaited the answer. Unknown to me, he did not offer Terry much hope for my survival. He said, "I have seen many cases like this one. The cancer has usually has spread to the lymph system. In that case it is terminal. Needless to say this made Terri frantic. But she kept it from me. The biopsy results came back a few days later. Happily the results were negative. We breathed a sigh of relief. Hers was deeper than mine because of her secret. This time a high hurdle had been cleared. Again I felt there could be none higher.

My convalescent period lasted three weeks in the hospital. Hospital personnel wanted to put me in a nursing home. They went ahead making arrangements without our consent. For days, Terri had a knock-down drag-out fight with the woman in charge of after care. The woman's point was Terri could not care for me due to my almost complete immobility. Terri would not hear of it. She said that she would manage. There would be no nursing home for her baby. Terri always fought for her family members. So, home I went. For several weeks I had a visiting nurse, a male physical (PT) and a female occupational therapist (OT) at my home. There was also an aide to wash me. The trauma of the operation left my right side almost completely paralyzed. I could only raise my right arm about 1 inch off the bed. My neurologist blamed it on the affect of the anesthetic on my MS or just the trauma of the operation. Many workouts with the OT partially restored the use of my right limbs. Terri was so happy when that happened that she gave the OT a big hug. But my dexterity and mobility never returned to the condition prior to the operation which was sub-par beforehand. Now I had to burden Terri with more work. Not only was it work but it was gross work. She had to clean out my ostomy bag 2-3 times per day. It was just another thing to increase my feelings of guilt and frustration. I expected to get Terri maids at this time of her life. Instead, I was making her a maid and a nurse. Although it was not my fault, I felt as guilty and frustrated as hell. My plans for her golden years were destroyed. When I would look out the window to see her taking out the heavy trash cans, I would cry. She had to do everything. Guilty only begins to describe how I felt.

Terri's health kept going downhill. Her hands were very cold, she would have occasional chest pains, and she fell asleep as soon as her head hit the pillow. This was not like her. All our life, she had always stayed up to watch the Tonight show. The guilt I was feeling increased. She was doing too much for me when she needed care as much or more than I did. I volunteered several times to go into a nursing home to take the pressure off her. She would not hear of it. She said, "You were always a good husband and father, so I'll do it. I won't pretend I like it, but when I feel, good, I don't mind at all." Not many men are lucky enough to get a wife like Terri.

To brighten our lives my daughter Terri then had a beautiful baby girl named Cassidy. One of the highlights of my wife's life was seeing the birth. Ten days later Tiffany had a cute baby boy named Lucas. A couple of weeks later my wife began to watch little Cassidy for two hours per day. This was the result of my daughter working days and her husband working nights. My wife watched her for the two hours between their shifts. Terri really bonded with the baby. She loved Cassidy like she was her own. So did I. Madison and now Cassidy were apples of my eye. Six months later Diane had a cute baby boy named Tom. We were now rich with young grandchildren. This greatly pleased Terri who always loved children. We now had a total of eleven grandchildren. My daughter began to worry about her mom's health. She offered to make other arrangements for Cassidy's care. But Terri said, "Don't you dare. That's my only pleasure in life." I always teased her that Cassidy took my place as the love of her life. She would answer, "Yep."

Since I first got MS Terri's personality had changed. She became a much stronger person. I am sure this was out of necessity. She now became the head of the household. She had to do absolutely everything with virtually no help. I knew how bitter she felt about the rapid change in our fate. She felt more badly for me than for herself. This was true even though she was the one saddled with all the work, bad health, no lover, etc.

During 2001 things became an increased effort for Terri. I did not notice it at first because Terri always let out a big sigh when she did something physical. But then it became very noticeable that she was laboring when carrying home groceries. I told her to stop buying bottled water and soda. Then she would leave the bags outside for Bill to bring in when he brought Cassidy in the afternoon. I did not think much of it at the time. I just assumed the bags were extra heavy. But then a couple of months later she had trouble walking up our slightly inclined driveway. She would have chest pains and get out of breathe. At this time, Terry called together some of our children and a lawyer. The purpose was to make sure arrangements were made to care for me. Instead of worrying about her health, she wanted to make sure care would be taken of me. That is love for you. That was just like her. She was always worried about me or her children first.

For several years I had been nagging her to see a cardiologist, but she would not go. She happened to have an appointment at that time with her endocrinologist. He dismissed this problem simply saying she looked good. His wife was a cardiologist. He should have recognized the problem from a stethoscope exam. Hell I felt sure it was blocked arteries just from her problem coming up the drive way. Yet he seemed to dismiss it. We knew better than what the doctor said and sent her to my cousin's cardiology group. They diagnosed it as heart failure. They put her in a second rate hospital where they ran some tests. She did not like the attending physician. To this day we never received results of those tests. She could not get the physician to give answers so she got herself dismissed. After a week of hearing nothing from them, she decided through friends to go to a top-notch cardiologist. They knew him well and he was located at a grade A hospital in Philadelphia. Terri was scheduled for a catherization. After forty nine years we new each other well. She was scared to death but tried to hide it. That morning when she left for her test she kissed me many times and said, "Don't worry, I'm too mean to die." Then her true feelings surfaced when she showed me the outfit she wanted to wear for burial. That is the last time I saw her. On the way to the hospital she told her friend, "I think I waited too long." The test revealed she had seven blocked arteries. They were 95% blocked. She needed immediate quadruple by-pass surgery. She called me the night before the surgery. She always asked my advice on something this important. This time she did not. I can only speculate that the doctor convinced her it would be fatal soon to not have it done. I feel sure she felt the chances of surviving it were slim with her diabetes and thyroid problems. If I know her, she did not want to saddle me with giving her lose-lose advice. The night before the operation she called to tell me she had to have it and that was that. That is the last time I spoke to her. If I would have known that would be the last time there is so much more I wanted to tell her. I am so sorry I did not reiterate how much she meant to me and how much I loved her.

She had the operation and at first it seemed to be successful. The next day she was sitting up in bed talking to visitors. I breathed a sigh of relief and was thinking of going to visit. Then she suddenly and steadily went down hill. My daughter Rosie tells me her first words every day were, "How's daddy doing." Evidently she was allergic to Heparin. She died of

Heparin induced thrombocytopenia. She went in for a test and I never saw her again. That haunts me till today. It also bothers me that I was not there at the end to comfort her. But my kids tell me the bed was so high that I could never even see her from my wheel chair. Also, if I came she probably would have suspected it was the end. At first the doctors thought they could save her life by amputating her leg. When asked she agreed. But I had the power of attorney under her living will. If I know Terri, when she recuperated, she would have hated anyone who did that to her. In fact, her best friend came over to my house and begged me to let her go since she had so many things wrong with her. I felt the friend was correct, but I could not pull the trigger even though Terri always told me to never let her be deformed. While I was trying to decide, she expired.

This is the one hurdle I can never get over. It is just too high for me. I always told Terri that if she died first I would not be far behind. She would always tell me I have all the kids and grandkids to occupy me. At the time, I did not think that would be enough. When she died I thought my life had ended. But all the kids have been wonderful to me. They helped me survive this. I feel closer to them now than at any time in my life. The grandchildren are wonderful too, especially the young ones. Watching all these kids, I see reminders of Terri in habits and looks.

A couple of months later I went to see her grave. I looked down and thought I hope you know how much I love you. Then I thought each of us always knew that.

CHAPTER 12

TERRI AND LIFE WITHOUT HER

This could be a very short chapter because I have very little life without Terri. Due to my incapacities it consists mostly of sitting in front of a computer playing card games, writing books which proved I was not a novelist and playing fantasy sports. My once rich life ended rather abruptly in 1984. I thought it was surely completely ended when Terri died. We were that devoted and attached to each other. After all we were partners for forty-nine years. I was completely lost and truly broken-hearted without her. I had no really close friends through most of my life. Terri was my only close friend. I lived so far from work and was a supervisor 2/3 of my career so I could not develop close friendships there. Most of my spare time was spent working in scouts and little league. I only had acquaintances there. My only close friends were the

Bards who took Terri and me out very often when all others deserted us. They were getting old now so I did not want them to have to deal with taking fat me out. Besides I had no desire to go out. My future life looked dismal to me. But as Terri predicted my kids and their kids helped me through this trying time.

To add to my heart break the world had changed so much since I was young, I felt like I no longer belonged in it. I was lucky enough to grow up in the '50's. Things were a lot calmer back then. The TV show was accurately named *HAPPY DAYS*. There were almost no drugs and very little murders. No drive by shootings. There were no computers with websites and chat rooms where young kids could fall prey to sexual predators. There were no Columbines or other school shootings like today. I never remember a mother murdering her children. There were no riots among elementary school children. Things were certainly different.

Although rock and roll was beginning to come into vogue in the '50's. Most of the popular music was love ballads. The music of the day seems to set the tone for the times. On came acid rock and drugs. This was followed by the sexual revolution and free love. The morals of the country began to decay. Women began to bare their breasts for rock bands. I guess I am a prude. I could not tolerate this. Terri and I were our only sex partners all our lives. I would not want it any other way. We found it very calming and warming to completely belong to each other. In my day you were lucky to get a good-night kiss on your first date with a girl. Today many couples have sex on their first date. Women had more respect for themselves than those of today. I think today's girls are losing out. After thinking about my situation I had to conclude that not only was I very lucky to live in those times. I was even luckier to have such a loving and devoted wife. Considering her illnesses and multiple pregnancies, my luck was extended to have her for as long as I did. I was indeed very lucky. We were glued together through three years of courtship and forty six and a half years of marriage. My luck ran out when I got my diseases. Although I hated to have to retire early with a disabling disease, there was some gratification with my plight. I got to spend full time with Terri for the last eighteen years of her life. That was very enjoyable. I would not trade that for anything.

Through most of this book I portrayed Terri as sort of a saint. That is because to me she was a saint. But like all of us she had her faults. Our children viewed her differently than I did. This is a natural consequence of our differing relationships. From when they were young children, Terri was their main disciplinarian since I was at school or work most of the time. Then too I tried to never argue with her over punishments in front of them. We discussed them in private. That is why some of her way out punishments were greatly reduced overnight. My children probably think I spoiled her and kept quiet too often. I am sure that is true and for her sake and mine, I am glad I did. For their sake I may have been a failure. The kids probably think I never stood up for them. I did behind closed doors. Funny but Terri thought I never stood up for her in her conflicts with the kids. These conflicts were the reason for most of the arguments in our married life.

As I said before no one is perfect. We all have faults. Among her biggest faults were; her temper which often made her words escape before her brain functioned, she would never admit she was wrong and almost never said she was sorry. These faults were trivial to me but bothered others, especially our children. But her faults should be weighed against her many attributes. She was a truly genuine person. What you saw is what you got. She was a loving, unselfish and overly generous person. She was always the first to volunteer a helping hand to a relative or friend in need. She did this despite being sick most of her life. She would never complain about the severity of her illnesses because as she said, "Nobody wants to hear it, they have their own problems." She would have given her life for me or any of her children. It hurt her when many people she helped never reciprocated. And I mean never. Some viewed this as a fault. But she really wanted to know her efforts were appreciated.

Soon after Terri died we went through her belongings and found a variety of clothes and shoes estimated at $25,000.00.

They were of all different sizes. Her weight fluctuated so much due to her thyroid problem until it was eradicated. Just before it was eradicated she lost 23 pounds in one week. After the eradication she had to take the synthetic thyroxin, Synthroid, for the rest of her life. In hope of losing the weight she often bought smaller sizes on sale. But the loss did not come. In the last three to four years I believe it was more because of her eating habits than her gland. Many of the clothes we found were never worn. They still had the price tags on them. She was an avid sales shopper. Finding great sales was a thing she loved in her latter years. In fact, she bought many duplicate appliances when she found great sales. These actually saved us money in the long run. In the last several years she had little else to make her happy. I was actually thrilled to pay for this pleasure for her. For I could always be sure she would never spend more than we could afford. I was the spendthrift of our duo.

As I said earlier I felt very guilty of the obvious pain I was causing Terri. To ease my guilt feelings and give her some relief I insisted she have some getaways. She would not go because of money. Then I made some money in the stock market and insisted she go. She visited a friend in Florida twice, went to Disney world with another friend and finally I forced her to go to Las Vegas with a few of the neighborhood women. This was all to get her away from the drudgery of caring for me. After each trip I could see a marked improvement in her whole demeanor. This thrilled me as much as if I went.

A couple of months after she died I sold my house. I could not stand the thought of living there with all those memories. I went to live with Tom and Diane because a] his house was large enough, b] we could make a room in the garage to put me on one floor without upsetting his home too much, c] Tom and I had the most in common and d] Diane did not work so I would not be alone all day. She seemed perfectly willing to accept me. I had to stay in my house with all the memories it had for me until my room was built. During those months, all my children helped me survive our loss. I felt so damned "all alone" and like my heart was broken beyond repair. But a little at a time my kids helped me get better. Just their presence was enough. But they also helped in varying degrees to do the gross job of changing my ostomy bag. On weekend mornings they dressed me. At night they undressed me and put me to bed. Fortunately, I had paid help to wash and dress me on weekday mornings.

During the last couple of years of her life Terri was very unhappy with our existence. She felt we had no life and were waiting to die. It certainly seemed the same to me. She met her demise and now I was awaiting mine. I still continually rewind and replay the last week of Terri's life in my mind. I see her smiling face, feel her kisses and hear her saying "don't worry, I'm too mean to die." Her death has had a lasting effect on me. I have to be careful which TV shows I watch now. Seeing dying people in hospital shows has an adverse effect on me. Shows with tender love scenes make me cry too. Shows that Terri and I would particularly enjoy together have the same effect. When she first died I found myself looking out the window for her. Then every time the front door opened I would think it was her. Almost four years later, I still look over to her non-existent bed to see if the sound of my electric bed is bothering her. A couple of times I found myself talking to her when I was not fully awake yet. When I hear an airplane passing overhead, I remember returning home from business trips. When the plane would pass over Cherry Hill a loving anxiety filled me. I anxiously awaited landing so I could quickly drive home. There I knew Terri's warm embraces and kisses awaited me. This was the best part o my trips. All of this is the lasting effect of being married to such a loving devoted person. I hope this writing got across that she was a truly genuine, caring and thoughtful person. She was to everyone. She was the first to volunteer help to family or friends whenever they needed it. It did not matter how difficult it was or how she felt at the time. Although she was a physical weakling, she was fearless. She exemplified the saying "IT'S NOT THE SIZE OF THE DOG IN THE FIGHT. IT'S THE SIZE OF THE FIGHT IN THE DOG." I remember how she fooled a couple of merchants into replacing inferior products for us and our daughter. Gary Papa was a well known sportscaster on the channel six's action news. When the merchants would not replace the products, she told them she would tell her nephew Gary. Then they could hear all about it on the news. The merchants then granted her request.

Terri was a devoted wife and nursed me through my gross illnesses when many other women would have left. We had forty-nine wonderful loving years together, forty-six married. I will miss her with a broken-heart till the day I die. I have survived longer than I thought I would thanks to the efforts of my kids and the cute loving faces of our grandchildren.

There were some significant events since her death. First, our 12th grandchild was born to Diane and Tom. Like all our grandchildren he is an absolute cutie. I just know he would have had a great impact on Terri because he is the image of his father when Tom was a baby. Shortly thereafter my brother Johnny died from a tumor on the pituitary gland. This did not come as a shock because I knew of his condition and the kind of life he led. The next event was the devastating news that Cassidy was diabetic and had to take insulin. Terri had bonded closely with Cass when she sat for her. I just know the news would have devastated Terri. She would have felt like she gave it to her. But Bill's brother had diabetes too. Genetics were against her too. The next significant event was the terrible shocking news my youngest brother Albert died of a heart attack at only fifty-two years of age. This happened just as we were about to mend fences. As I thought about this

I recalled that my brother looked and had the mannerisms of my mother's three nephews that also died of heart attacks in their early fifties. It seems genetics was at work again. I did get to meet his two sons for the first time. Even though the oldest, Chris, was fourteen. Chris proved to be all the good things I heard about him. But he suffered from the same as his father. He was a Pittsburgh Pirates fan. Then we got more bad news. My grandson Lucas had Juvenile Diabetes too. This, I am sure, would have hit Terri very hard as would have Cassidy's diagnosis. But it was genetics at work again. Both of Lucas' parents had diabetes in their families.

Although all my children have been good to me and helped me survive, Tom and especially Diane have been exceptional. She puts up with me and takes care of my everyday needs. She has been vital to my survival. I will forever be thankful to all my children but especially to Tom and most especially to Diane.

EPILOG

Despite all my problems, I had a happy life. First I was lucky enough to meet the girl for me. She was truly a devoted and loving wife. Then we had a life-long story book romance. There were many accomplishments for me. Wanting to do good for Terri got me off my butt to make something of myself. The song *GOD ONLY KNOWS WHERE I'D BE WITHOUT YOU* seems fitting. My success was not because I was exceptionally smart but from hard work. As my graduate professor once told me, you are not nearly the smartest student I ever had but you have the best intuition or knack for chemistry. If there is such a thing as reincarnation, I must have been a chemist in my former life.

But my greatest accomplishment is shared by Terri. It's how are children turned out. She has to get most of the credit for it. First, she carried and bore them. Then, she raised them much more than I did. They owe what they are mainly to her. We always tried to make them independent and self-sufficient like we were. They all turned out that way either because of the way we raised them or it was inborn in them. Today they are all successful in their chosen careers. I am very proud of each and every one of them as was their mom.

ABOUT THE AUTHOR

Louis J. Papa holds a BA degree from Temple University and a Ph.D. from the University of North Carolina. Both degrees are in Chemistry. He spent his entire career doing research at DuPont. During his combined careers at UNC and DuPont he authored chapters in three technical books, a chemical dictionary and fourteen technical research articles in scientific journals. He is listed in *Who is Who in American Men of Science.* The author is now retired on disability suffering from multiple sclerosis. This forced retirement gave him time to pursue a life long desire to write novels. He did this even though confined to a wheel chair and only able to type with one finger. He already has published three books: *A Backward Life, Playing the Hand I was Dealt* and *Life on the Edge.*

LaVergne, TN USA
13 November 2009
163948LV00001B/260/A